MATHS

FOR PRACTICE & REVISION

1

DECIMALS

FRACTIONS

PERCENTAGE

PETER ROBSON

Srij

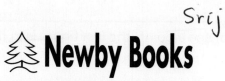

Newby Books

EASINGWOLD TOWN HALL COMPANY LTD
THE ADVERTISER OFFICE, MARKET PLACE,
EASINGWOLD, YORK YO61 3AB
TEL 01347 821329
www.newbybooks.co.uk

A DECIMAL COLUMNS

Learn the names of the columns

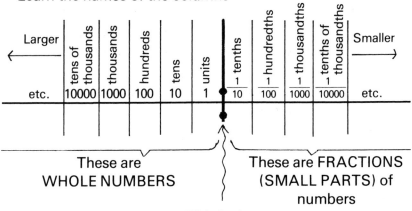

Larger	tens of thousands	thousands	hundreds	tens	units	tenths	hundredths	thousandths	tenths of thousandths	Smaller
etc.	10000	1000	100	10	1	$\frac{1}{10}$	$\frac{1}{100}$	$\frac{1}{1000}$	$\frac{1}{10000}$	etc.

These are
WHOLE NUMBERS

These are FRACTIONS
(SMALL PARTS) of
numbers

This is the
DECIMAL POINT

B Writing decimal numbers

*Always look for the POINT. This tells you in which columns to put the numbers.

*The UNITS (ones) column is always just to the LEFT of the point.

e.g. (1)   37.450

e.g. (2)   0.0728

 If you cannot see a point, the last figure is in the UNITS column

e.g.   629

a

Draw decimal columns down your page

etc.

and write each of these numbers in the correct columns.
Always look first for the POINT or the UNITS column.

1) 32.86	5) 0.671	9) 86.5	13) 15
2) 1.507	6) 500.3	10) 4.8821	14) 23.056
3) 924.2	7) 1.012	11) 0.7	15) 0.008
4) 511.85	8) 970	12) 362.98	

---

b

Copy these numbers, and in each number underline the figure
which is in the UNITS column
e.g.   428.95 = 428.95

1) 59.8	5) 4624.5	9) 5.82	13) 0.0042
2) 6.510	6) 3.9785	10) 113.07	14) 60.0
3) 322.7	7) 7100	11) 6	15) 0.1
4) 1.4	8) 0.052	12) 739.135	

---

c

Draw decimal columns and write these numbers correctly.
For each of the numbers give the NAME of the column which
has a figure 4, e.g.

30.42 | | 3 | 0 ⦙ 4 | 2 | | 4 is in the TENTHS column

1) 14.3	4) 174	7) 0.401	9) 4990
2) 548.5	5) 0.346	8) 47.8	10) 5.324
3) 9.4	6) 428.5		

---

d

Copy these numbers, and for each number give the name of the
column which has a figure 7

1) 372.5	4) 3.447	7) 0.788	9) 4733
2) 17.32	5) 7	8) 7654.0	10) 71.5
3) 66.175	6) 5.78		

A ✚ ADDITION

e.g. (1) 5.78 + 4 + 16.5

*1) Make quite sure you know
where the POINT is
in each number 5.78 + 4.0 + 16.5

REMEMBER 8 is 8.0
23 is 23.0
6 is 6.0, etc

*2) Write a row of points
one underneath the other

```
      .
      .
      .
  _____
      .
```

*3) Fit numbers carefully
in correct columns

```
    5.78
    4.0
+  16.5
  _____
     .
```

*4) Add, being sure to put
the point in your answer

```
    5.78
    4.0
+  16.5
  _____
   26.28
```

---

e.g. (2) 14.64 + 7.2 + 5.125 + 12

```
    14.64
     7.2
     5.125
+   12.0
   _____
    38.965
```

a Make these numbers look more like decimals
(e.g.   7 = 7.0,   13 = 13.0)

1) 8	6) 32	11) 14	16) 67
2) 24	7) 1	12) 53	17) 312
3) 16	8) 125	13) 2	18) 18
4) 5	9) 6	14) 42	19) 650
5) 9	10) 47	15) 3000	20) 111

---

b Try these additions

1) 6.2 + 5.6	6) 6.8 + 2.93 + 11.15
2) 12.5 + 7.8	7) 3.75 + 9.4 + 1.06
3) 3.9 + 5.3	8) 65.07 + 24.5 + 1.25
4) 5.28 + 9.76	9) 7.49 + 14 + 3.8
5) 4.3 + 6.28	10) 32 + 14.5 + 6.75

---

c Find the SUM (adding) of each of these groups of numbers

1) 25.85, 6.66, 3.2	6) 9.68, 3.71, 12.9
2) 53, 8.2, 0.8	7) 75.2, 6.84, 0.325
3) 5.4, 3.2, 7.8, 0.3	8) 184, 36.9, 20.5
4) 6.72, 12.8, 2.17	9) 0.3, 0.0075, 0.014
5) 17, 12.6, 4.58	10) 8.85, 85, 5.585

---

d Find the sum of each of these groups

1) 4.235, 0.52, 8.475	6) 99.9, 999, 9.99
2) 1350, 75.5, 623.25	7) 1.27, 3.49, 12.85, 3.2
3) 0.007, 0.083, 0.129	8) 87.55, 5.235, 119
4) 4.03, 0.084, 19.1	9) 0.00082, 0.0064, 0.0001
5) 27, 14.95, 8	10) 6.2, 34.8, 7.5, 1.15

A —— SUBTRACTION

e.g. (1)   6 − 1.84

*1) Make quite sure you know
where the POINT is in each
number

REMEMBER   12   is   12.0
         5   is   5.0
             etc.

$$6.0 - 1.84$$

*2) Write a row of points
one underneath the other

.
—.—
.

*3) Fit numbers carefully
in correct columns

    6.0
−   1.84
     .

*4) FILL IN ANY SPACES
WITH NOUGHTS

    6.00
−   1.84
     .

*5) Subtract (take away),
being sure to put the point
in your answer

    6.00
−   1.84
    4.16

---

e.g. (2) Subtract 3.52 from 12.7

    12.70
−   3.52
     9.18

The number you are subtracting
always goes at the bottom.

a Make these numbers look more like decimals
(e.g.   24 = 24.0,   8 = 8.0)

1) 3	3) 62	5) 413	7) 5	9) 1000
2) 74	4) 9	6) 14	8) 87	10) 28

b
1) 8.7 − 4.2	6) 14.2 − 7.8	11) 17.51 − 4.9
2) 16.3 − 11.1	7) 0.37 − 0.29	12) 0.012 − 0.005
3) 9.6 − 6.1	8) 5.38 − 3.64	13) 8.25 − 5
4) 25.8 − 14.8	9) 21.3 − 2.8	14) 3.805 − 1.062
5) 7.6 − 2.3	10) 6.23 − 1.8	15) 20.0 − 3.8

c Remember to fill in spaces with noughts if necessary

1) 15.2 − 8.4	6) 6.19 − 6.045	11) 62 − 14.32
2) 4.3 − 1.9	7) 9.07 − 7.8	12) 5.482 − 3.917
3) 6.7 − 1.46	8) 42.5 − 7.36	13) 22.2 − 4.56
4) 32.45 − 15.7	9) 0.306 − 0.04	14) 10.03 − 8.8
5) 28 − 4.6	10) 1.5 − 0.75	15) 0.9 − 0.07

d
1) 34.5 − 22.2	11) From 8.3 subtract 1.7
2) 6.27 − 4.8	12) From 13.13 subtract 1.313
3) 0.325 − 0.29	13) From 94 subtract 4.9
4) 9.50 − 1.77	14) From 5.32 subtract 0.48
5) 40 − 12.5	15) Find the difference between 18.1 and 2.7
6) 1.35 − 1.275	16) Find the difference between 0.03 and 0.011
7) 6.28 − 0.08	17) Find the difference between 47.5 and 38.0
8) 53.1 − 7.63	18) Subtract 3.47 from 11.08
9) 0.0006 − 0.00002	19) Subtract 0.99 from 1
10) 20 − 14.28	20) Subtract 3.55 from 22.3

A $+$ $-$ ADDITION & SUBTRACTION

e.g. $9.8 + 3.6 - 4.72$

*Do each part SEPARATELY
(unless all the signs are $+$)

$$
\begin{array}{r}
9.8 \\
+ \quad 3.6 \\
\hline
13.4 \\
\hline
\end{array}
$$

Then

$$
\begin{array}{r}
13.40 \\
- \quad 4.72 \\
\hline
8.68 \\
\end{array}
$$

---

e.g. (2)

$$24 - 5.87 - 3.5$$

$$
\begin{array}{r}
24.00 \\
- \quad 5.87 \\
\hline
18.13 \\
- \quad 3.5 \\
\hline
14.63 \\
\end{array}
$$

e.g. (3)

$$62.5 - 46.9 + 25.4$$

$$
\begin{array}{r}
62.5 \\
- \quad 46.9 \\
\hline
15.6 \\
+ \quad 25.4 \\
\hline
41.0 \\
\end{array}
\qquad \text{or} \qquad
\begin{array}{r}
62.5 \\
+ \quad 25.4 \\
\hline
87.9 \\
- \quad 46.9 \\
\hline
41.0 \\
\end{array}
$$

B Brackets

e.g. $15.43 - (2.97 + 3.58)$

*1) Always do the parts
   INSIDE the brackets first

$$
\begin{array}{r}
2.97 \\
+ \quad 3.58 \\
\hline
6.55 \\
\hline
\end{array}
$$

*2) Then do the other parts

$$
\begin{array}{r}
15.43 \\
- \quad 6.55 \\
\hline
8.88 \\
\end{array}
$$

a

1) 5.62 + 2.17	6) 3.258 + 0.07	11) 27.5 + 27.5
2) 32.6 − 12.2	7) 15 − 9.73	12) 8.27 + 6 + 7.8
3) 1.43 + 18.8	8) 88.8 + 8.888	13) 14.22 − 5.075
4) 6 + 2.3 + 5.9	9) 6.7 − 2.14	14) 0.94 + 0.094
5) 30.2 − 19.3	10) 2 − 0.003	15) 100 − 82.3

b

1) 6.4 + 2.3 − 5.2	6) 2.9 + 5.5 − 8.3
2) 27 + 4.9 − 16.7	7) 7.8 − 2.1 − 3.4
3) 0.32 + 0.57 − 0.48	8) 50.5 − 23.6 + 8.4
4) 9.8 + 3.9 − 7.8	9) 0.911 + 0.747 + 0.208
5) 56.1 + 43.9 − 80.0	10) 1.7 + 5.6 − 4.25

c

If there are brackets, remember to do the part in brackets first

1) 4.32 + 3.57 − 5.46	6) (7.4 + 14.1) − (17.9 + 1.8)
2) 16.9 − (10.5 + 4.1)	7) 9.03 − 2.75 − 1.96
3) 0.372 + 0.088 − 0.163	8) 46 − (13.6 + 23.7)
4) 9.43 − (2.17 + 5.34)	9) 0.292 + 0.545 − 0.837
5) 3.785 + 6.87 + 9.345	10) 9.8 − (3 + 1.9 + 4.65)

d

1) Add 18.5 to 16.9 and subtract 20.7
2) From the sum of 0.58 and 2.9 subtract 3
3) From 7.4 subtract the sum of 3.7 and 2.9
4) Add 1.006 to 2.013 and subtract 0.92 from the result
5) Subtract the sum of 25.9 and 17.8 from 50
6) From the sum of 1.05, 2.6 and 0.87, subtract 4.015
7) Subtract 4.9 from the sum of 3.08 and 2.97
8) From 7 subtract 1.7 and then subtract 0.17
9) Subtract the sum of 6.4 and 2.5 from the sum of 7.8 and 5.6
10) Find the difference between 7.6 and the sum of 3.2 and 8.2

✕ MULTIPLICATION BY 10, 100, 1000, ETC.

NOTICE that the **POINT DOES NOT MOVE** and the **FIGURES STAY THE SAME** (except for an extra nought now and then)

 MULTIPLY BY 10
*Move the number .
    ONE PLACE LARGER

e.g   2.378 × 10
         23.78

e.g.   4.03 × 10
         40.3

 MULTIPLY BY 100
*Move the number
    TWO PLACES LARGER

e.g.   5.194 × 100
         519.4

e.g.   16.7 × 100
         167**0**

REMEMBER — Fill up to the point with noughts

 MULTIPLY BY 1000
*Move the number
    THREE PLACES LARGER

e.g.   0.2437 × 1000
         243.7

e.g.   5.4 × 1000
         54**00**

REMEMBER — Fill up to the point with noughts

E (1) It is better to write 0.34 than .34
      The nought helps to show where the point is.
(2) How would you multiply by 10000 or 100000?

a

Write these numbers and then multiply each of them by 10

1) 1.35	6) 0.395	11) 37.55	16) 4618.5
2) 29.78	7) 67.14	12) 4.683	17) 0.032
3) 4.657	8) 1.0567	13) 9	18) 97.58
4) 209.3	9) 733.2	14) 0.008	19) 2.003
5) 58	10) 0.24	15) 1.07	20) 0.101

b

Write these numbers and multiply each of them by 100

1) 1.438	6) 54.81	11) 0.6473	16) 4.8181
2) 29.52	7) 663.5	12) 58.2	17) 62.9
3) 0.327	8) 49.380	13) 708.05	18) 91.78
4) 74	9) 6.5055	14) 2.039	19) 0.0013
5) 16.585	10) 8	15) 0.0328	20) 5.55555

c

Write these numbers and multiply each of them by 1000

1) 6.5382	6) 89.87	11) 5.3900	16) 0.0084
2) 0.00253	7) 34.5678	12) 7.83	17) 62.052
3) 14.725	8) 0.921	13) 638	18) 3.9
4) 9.3008	9) 2	14) 2.4193	19) 68.75
5) 16	10) 68.44	15) 16.1	20) 0.012

d

Try these

1) 5.13 × 10	8) 88.57 × 10	15) 69.57 × 10
2) 0.627 × 100	9) 2.148 × 1000	16) 28.34 × 1000
3) 33.485 × 10	10) 53 × 100	17) 413.705 × 100
4) 1.5945 × 1000	11) 145.7 × 1000	18) 74 × 1000
5) 8 × 10	12) 12.5 × 100	19) 0.0032 × 10
6) 6.352 × 100	13) 0.79 × 10	20) 99.8 × 100
7) 0.00004 × 1000	14) 2.48 × 100	

✕ MULTIPLICATION e.g.   62.9 ×   0.7

*1) Write out the question,
underlining decimal places
(figures after the point)   62.<u>9</u> ×   0.<u>7</u>

*2) Set out as a multiplication
but WITHOUT THE POINTS.   629
Miss out any LEFT-HAND   ×   7
noughts.

*3) Work out   629
                                                ×   7
                                              ‾‾‾‾
                                                4403

*4) Look back at the question
and count the decimal places.
Your answer should have the
SAME NUMBER OF DECIMAL   62.<u>9</u> ×   0.<u>7</u>
PLACES as the question.   =   44.<u>03</u>

B Long multiplication works out   e.g.   2.<u>78</u> ×   4.<u>2</u>
just the same way

                                                278
                                            ×   42
                                          ‾‾‾‾‾‾
                                              556
                                            1112
                                          ‾‾‾‾‾‾
                                            11676

                        So   2.<u>78</u> × 4.<u>2</u> = 11.<u>676</u>

C Fill up to the point with noughts
if necessary   e.g.   0.<u>16</u> ×   0.<u>3</u>
                                            16
                                        ×   3
                                        ‾‾‾‾   0.16 × 0.3 =
                                            48   . _<u>48</u>
                            so answer is   0.0<u>48</u>

D It is better to write 0.942 than .942
The nought helps to show where the point is.

a

Decimal places have been underlined to help you

1) 6.2 × 3
2) 3.8 × 0.2
3) 9.2 × 4
4) 5.7 × 0.5
5) 2.35 × 6

6) 3.44 × 0.7
7) 2.06 × 0.8
8) 1.25 × 2
9) 39.2 × 0.3
10) 4.7 × 0.05

11) 5.19 × 0.4
12) 2.3 × 11
13) 92.3 × 0.07
14) 4.8 × 2.1
15) 16.75 × 0.6

---

b

Remember to fill up to the point with noughts if necessary

1) 2.43 × 0.9
2) 1.42 × 0.03
3) 2.7 × 3.4
4) 7.45 × 0.27
5) 0.62 × 5.5

6) 1.236 × 0.04
7) 0.08 × 0.5
8) 3.91 × 24
9) 62.05 × 3.6
10) 2.51 × 67

11) 0.175 × 0.06
12) 54.4 × 1.8
13) 0.38 × 0.14
14) 0.085 × 0.062
15) 93.7 × 0.81

---

c

1) 5.72 × 0.8
2) 6.47 × 2.3
3) 2.07 × 1.06
4) 9.9 × 9.9
5) 0.28 × 0.3

6) 0.68 × 29
7) 1.052 × 9.6
8) 67.5 × 0.08
9) 0.329 × 0.2
10) 0.008 × 0.09

11) 7.77 × 0.55
12) 0.042 × 63
13) 613 × 400
14) 2.08 × 1.35
15) 343.4 × 0.061

---

d

1) Multiply 24.8 by 6
2) Multiply 6.9 by 3.2
3) Multiply 2.075 by 8
4) Multiply 5.15 by 0.05
5) Multiply 94 by 0.1

6) Multiply 7.56 by 0.21
7) Multiply 2.22 by 7.3
8) Multiply 0.59 by 82
9) Multiply 0.27 by 0.004
10) Multiply 4.06 by 3.002

11) Find the product of 1.023 and 0.97
12) Find the product of 1.55 and 7.4
13) Find the product of 0.69 and 0.36
14) Find the product of 7.5 and 0.0003
15) Find the product of 0.28 and 0.28

A ÷ DIVISION BY 10, 100, 1000, ETC.

NOTICE that the POINT DOES NOT MOVE and the FIGURES
STAY THE SAME (except for an extra nought now and then)

 DIVIDE BY 10
*Move the number
ONE PLACE SMALLER

e.g.   43.6 ÷ 10

         4.36

e.g.   2.87 ÷ 10

      0.287

 DIVIDE BY 100
*Move the number
TWO PLACES SMALLER

e.g.   359.6 ÷ 100

        3.596

e.g.   1.49 ÷ 100

      0.**0**149

REMEMBER — Fill up to the point with noughts.

 DIVIDE BY 1000
*Move the number
THREE PLACES SMALLER

e.g.   10257   ÷   1000

        10.257

e.g.   35.49 ÷ 1000

      0.03549

REMEMBER — Fill up to the point with noughts

E

(1)   It is better to write 0.537 than .537
      The nought helps to show where the point is

(2)   How would you divide by 10000 or 100000?

a Write these numbers and then divide each of them by 10

1) 12.3	6) 9.85	11) 7538.5	16) 600.85
2) 25.69	7) 572.7	12) 0.037	17) 0.9
3) 438.1	8) 0.328	13) 50.03	18) 36.012
4) 73.892	9) 11.8904	14) 926	19) 0.0006
5) 2134.6	10) 8	15) 0.051	20) 74

b Write these numbers and divide each of them by 100

1) 327.8	6) 537.9	11) 200.5	16) 40358
2) 119.02	7) 2.83	12) 81	17) 329.747
3) 6845.5	8) 14.625	13) 999	18) 4
4) 23.48	9) 0.5	14) 1607.8	19) 21.3
5) 700	10) 7342	15) 56.65	20) 0.08

c Write these numbers and divide each of them by 1000

1) 5167.5	6) 159.20	11) 72000	16) 144.85
2) 23480.6	7) 67.84	12) 295.75	17) 0.78
3) 5000	8) 1243.7	13) 31	18) 203023
4) 917.8	9) 3008	14) 1469.02	19) 16.2
5) 3838.11	10) 972	15) 78.3	20) 9

d Try these

1) 892.3 ÷ 100	8) 0.65 ÷ 10	15) 66 ÷ 10
2) 417.5 ÷ 10	9) 5331 ÷ 100	16) 2.75 ÷ 100
3) 6 ÷ 10	10) 88888 ÷ 1000	17) 4 ÷ 1000
4) 3917.25 ÷ 1000	11) 95.62 ÷ 100	18) 537.2 ÷ 10
5) 488 ÷ 100	12) 3.44 ÷ 10	19) 495112 ÷ 1000
6) 36.4 ÷ 10	13) 0.8 ÷ 100	20) 0.06 ÷ 100
7) 773.8 ÷ 1000	14) 197 ÷ 1000	

 DIVISION by a whole number

e.g.   7.14 ÷ 3

*Keep the point in the ANSWER
above the point in the question

$$3\overline{)\,7.14}^{\,\cdot}$$

$$\begin{array}{r} 2.38 \\ 3\overline{)\,7.14} \end{array}$$

B RUNNING OUT OF NUMBERS

e.g. (1)   24.3 ÷ 5

*1) Do NOT put remainders at the
end of a decimal division

$$\begin{array}{r} 4.8\ ??? \\ 5\overline{)\,24.3} \end{array}$$

*2) ADD MORE NOUGHTS (as
many as you need) and keep
going

$$\begin{array}{r} 4.86 \\ 5\overline{)\,24.30} \end{array}$$

---

e.g (2)   2.9 ÷ 8

$$\begin{array}{r} 0.3\ ??? \\ 8\overline{)\,2.9} \end{array}$$

$$\begin{array}{r} 0.3625 \\ 8\overline{)\,2.9000} \end{array}$$

C RECURRING DECIMALS (Decimals which go on the same way for ever).

e.g. (1)   0.47 ÷ 3

$$\begin{array}{r} 0.1566666666\ \ \text{etc.} \\ 3\overline{)\,0.4700000000} \end{array}$$

The 6 goes on for ever, so write $0.15\dot{6}$

e.g. (2)   6.43 ÷ 11

$$\begin{array}{r} 0.58454545454 \\ 11\overline{)\,6.43000000000} \end{array}$$

The 45 goes on for ever, so write $0.58\dot{4}\dot{5}$

a

1) 5.22 ÷ 3	6) 58.3 ÷ 11	11) 6.72 ÷ 24
2) 742.5 ÷ 5	7) 11.12 ÷ 4	12) 446.5 ÷ 19
3) 0.516 ÷ 2	8) 0.048 ÷ 6	13) 0.1974 ÷ 21
4) 48.3 ÷ 7	9) 3.384 ÷ 9	14) 10.8 ÷ 12
5) 3.15 ÷ 3	10) 575.2 ÷ 8	15) 1.2062 ÷ 37

b

Remember to add NOUGHTS if you run out of numbers

1) 23.4 ÷ 5	6) 0.98 ÷ 5	11) 19.9 ÷ 16
2) 9.81 ÷ 6	7) 33.3 ÷ 2	12) 5.1 ÷ 12
3) 0.117 ÷ 2	8) 35.1 ÷ 8	13) 90.4 ÷ 25
4) 9.7 ÷ 8	9) 2.97 ÷ 6	14) 0.402 ÷ 24
5) 51.0 ÷ 4	10) 72.9 ÷ 4	15) 6.3 ÷ 15

c

The answers to these will be RECURRING DECIMALS

1) 22.3 ÷ 3	6) 100.6 ÷ 6	11) 44 ÷ 3
2) 14.6 ÷ 6	7) 5.79 ÷ 11	12) 0.94 ÷ 11
3) 6.84 ÷ 11	8) 0.885 ÷ 9	13) 100.0 ÷ 18
4) 2.2 ÷ 9	9) 2.0 ÷ 3	14) 36.7 ÷ 33
5) 5.6 ÷ 3	10) 31.6 ÷ 9	15) 23.2 ÷ 7

d

Try these (different sorts jumbled up)

1) 82.5 ÷ 3	6) 54.3 ÷ 8	11) 49.5 ÷ 11
2) 9.87 ÷ 2	7) 7.6 ÷ 6	12) 35.0 ÷ 12
3) 5.2 ÷ 11	8) 3.36 ÷ 7	13) 36.6 ÷ 15
4) 0.0124 ÷ 8	9) 0.69 ÷ 6	14) 105 ÷ 27
5) 3.002 ÷ 5	10) 6.1 ÷ 9	15) 0.343 ÷ 14

DIVISION by a decimal

*1) Write the question   e.g.   1.235 ÷ 0.05

*2) Make the RIGHT-HAND number
   into a whole number   ÷ 5
   (In this case you have to
   multiply it by 100)

*3) Move the LEFT-HAND number
   the same amount of places   123.5   ÷ 5
   (In this case, multiply it by
   100, too)

*4) Set out as usual, keeping the   .
   point in the answer directly   5) 123.5
   above the point in the question

                                              24.7
                                          5) 123.5

B   Examples of how to start

1)	3.69 ÷ 0.3	6)	0.0328 ÷ 0.006
	36.9 ÷ 3		32.8 ÷ 6

2)	43.55 ÷ 1.5	7)	7.2 ÷ 0.09
	435.5 ÷ 15		720 ÷ 9

3)	9.728 ÷ 0.04	8)	9.464 ÷ 0.26
	972.8 ÷ 4		946.4 ÷ 26

4)	41.6 ÷ 0.8	9)	0.5525 ÷ 0.17
	416 ÷ 8		55.25 ÷ 17

5)	258 ÷ 0.43	10)	62.5 ÷ 0.005
	25800 ÷ 43		62500 ÷ 5

a

1) 3.69 ÷ 0.3	*6)* 0.036 ÷ 0.6	*11)* 0.0052 ÷ 0.04
2) 42.5 ÷ 0.5	*7)* 1.77 ÷ 0.03	*12)* 5.275 ÷ 0.05
3) 0.632 ÷ 0.4	*8)* 26.8 ÷ 0.4	*13)* 5.275 ÷ 0.005
4) 5.04 ÷ 0.2	*9)* 1.82 ÷ 1.3	*14)* 0.0006 ÷ 0.002
5) 7.91 ÷ 0.7	*10)* 5.74 ÷ 1.4	*15)* 0.352 ÷ 0.11

---

b

1) 8.74 ÷ 0.1	*6)* 6.24 ÷ 0.5	*11)* 2.301 ÷ 0.3
2) 52.8 ÷ 0.02	*7)* 0.432 ÷ 1.8	*12)* 0.529 ÷ 2.3
3) 8.076 ÷ 0.4	*8)* 63.8 ÷ 1.1	*13)* 0.1234 ÷ 0.04
4) 54.4 ÷ 0.17	*9)* 0.5 ÷ 0.8	*14)* 132 ÷ 0.02
5) 8.25 ÷ 1.5	*10)* 38.08 ÷ 3.4	*15)* 46.8 ÷ 0.09

---

c

1) 3.26 ÷ 0.04	*6)* 96.6 ÷ 0.21	*11)* 0.0657 ÷ 0.9
2) 59 ÷ 0.5	*7)* 3.272 ÷ 0.8	*12)* 0.0036 ÷ 0.05
3) 10.2 ÷ 2	*8)* 72.4 ÷ 0.05	*13)* 40.66 ÷ 0.019
4) 85.8 ÷ 0.12	*9)* 37.6 ÷ 16	*14)* 594 ÷ 2.7
5) 18.24 ÷ 0.3	*10)* 4.64 ÷ 0.3	*15)* 0.0001 ÷ 0.02

---

d

1) Divide 1.56 by 0.4	*9)* Divide 6.252 by 0.03
2) Divide 28 by 0.5	*10)* Divide 1 by 0.9
3) Divide 0.408 by 1.2	*11)* Divide 149.1 by 0.07
4) Divide 28.5 by 30	*12)* Divide 0.896 by 1.28
5) Divide 38 by 0.8	*13)* Divide 3900 by 0.13
6) Divide 7.3 by 0.06	*14)* Divide 63.3 by 0.16
7) Divide 0.06 by 2.5	*15)* Divide 9.594 by 4.1
8) Divide 13.86 by 3.3	

✕ ➗ MULTIPLICATION AND DIVISION

*If there are two or more signs in the same question, DO EACH PART SEPARATELY

e.g. $4.35 \times 5.2 \div 0.4$

$4.35 \times 5.2 = 22.62$

Then $22.62 \div 0.4$

$= 56.55$

Brackets

*If there are brackets, always do the part INSIDE the brackets first

e.g. $14.4 \div (6.4 \times 0.05)$

$6.4 \times 0.05 = 0.32$

Then $14.4 \div 0.32$

$= 45$

$+ - \times \div$ MIXED DECIMALS

WITH BRACKETS

*1) Always do the part INSIDE the brackets first

*2) Then do the other parts

e.g. $4.41 \div (2.34 - 0.54)$

$2.34 - 0.54 = 1.8$

$4.41 \div 1.8$

$= 2.45$

WITHOUT BRACKETS

*1) Always do $\times$ or $\div$ first

*2) Then do $+$ or $-$

e.g. $3.27 + 3.4 \times 2.6$

$3.4 \times 2.6 = 8.84$

$3.27 + 8.84$

$= 12.11$

C REMEMBER 'B O M D A S'

First   **B**rackets

Then   **O**f, **M**ultiply, **D**ivide

Then   **A**dd, **S**ubtract

a

1) $9.4 \times 3.6 \div 2$
2) $66.5 \div 0.5 \div 0.7$
3) $1.7 \times 2.5 \times 4.2$
4) $0.207 \div (1.5 \times 0.6)$
5) $245 \times 0.01 \div 0.25$
6) $325 \times 0.2 \times 3.6$
7) $0.054 \times (3.84 \div 0.6)$
8) $0.8 \times 0.2 \div 0.005$
9) $4.9 \div 0.4 \times 0.7$
10) $0.465 \div (38.75 \times 0.8)$

b

1) $15.3 + 4.28$
2) 9.6×0.7
3) $46.1 - 12.8$
4) $5.5 \div 8$
5) 0.693×100
6) $0.523 - 0.085$
7) $7.38 + 65.904$
8) $4.068 \div 0.3$
9) $6.1 - 1.66$
10) 0.44×0.123
11) $335.8 \div 0.23$
12) 13×0.064
13) $90 - 5.16$
14) $82.82 + 8.282$
15) $0.624 \div 0.048$

c

1) $(0.62 + 1.6) \div 0.3$
2) $0.16 \times (9.3 - 1.55)$
3) $4.07 + 15.8 + 0.36$
4) $(0.0384 + 0.0615) \times 1000$
5) $0.98 \times 1.5 + 3.53$
6) $2.5 \times 2.5 \times 0.6$
7) $(0.11 - 0.0034) \div 1.3$
8) $132.3 + 44.4 - 167.6$
9) $2.115 \div 0.15 + 5.9$
10) $0.7474 - (20.2 \times 0.037)$
11) $(2.9 + 0.56) \times 1.5$
12) $0.59 \times (9.3 - 8.71)$
13) $35.30 - 7.38 - 26.93$
14) $22.14 \div (3.6 \times 0.05)$
15) $(5.05 - 4.95) \times (4.7 + 5.3)$

d

1) Subtract 0.76 from the sum of 8.69 and 2.73
2) Add 0.021 to the product of 0.14 and 0.7
3) Divide by 22 the sum of 0.55 and 0.99
4) Find the difference between (29×0.28) and $(3.73 \div 0.5)$
5) Multiply by 0.5 the difference between 133.3 and 27.2
6) Subtract 0.7 from the product of 64 and 0.025
7) Divide by 0.13 the difference between 0.53 and 0.14
8) Find the sum of 4.74, 474, 0.474 and 47.4
9) Multiply the product of 0.11 and 1.1 by 11
10) Add 8 to the difference between 4.50 and 2.51

A £ p MONEY

Money is worked out the same way as other decimals, but remember . . .

WHOLE POUNDS can be written with or without the decimal point

e.g. 'seventy-three pounds' can be written either £73 or £73.00

THE £ SIGN always comes BEFORE the amount
e.g. £639.00 (never 639.00£)

DECIMAL PLACES Money is written with TWO decimal places (never more and never less)

e.g. 'four pounds eighty' is written

£4.80 (never £4.8)

'sixteen pounds and fivepence' is written

£16.05 (never £16.5)

SMALL AMOUNTS, usually under £1, can be written in PENCE (p)

e.g. £0.67 can be written 67p

£0.08 can be written 8p

£0.93 can be written 93p

B CHANGING PENCE INTO POUNDS

e.g. Write in £ this amount 34p

*Divide by 100

34 ÷ 100

= £0.34

e.g. Write 9p in £

9 ÷ 100

= £0.09

To change **pounds** into **pence**, MULTIPLY by 100.

a Write these amounts in £

1) 82p	3) 7p	5) 125p	7) 6p	9) 10p
2) 23p	4) 99p	6) 2p	8) 50p	10) 1p

b

1) £3.27 + £4.88
2) £14.25 ÷ 3
3) £1.42 × 5
4) £8.27 − £3.74
5) £2.05 × 19
6) £16.38 + £23.91
7) £28.32 ÷ 12
8) £66.66 + £58.90
9) £6.50 − £1.74
10) 83p × 22
11) £94.50 ÷ 10
12) £43 + £25.75 + £4.55
13) £9.90 × 50
14) £2.24 + £1.88 − £3.25
15) £142 ÷ 8

c Calculate the change you should receive from a £5 note if you spend

1) £3.69	4) £2.58	7) £3.01	9) £4.44
2) £1.27	5) £4.61	8) £0.97	10) £2.72
3) £4.83	6) £1.99		

d

1) Find the cost of 6 railway tickets at £2.34 each
2) Add £14.72, £38.57, £5.84, £21.05
3) A man had £435.68. Then he spent £178.90. How much money did he have left?
4) Ann, Claire and Victoria shared equally £8.55. How much did each receive?
5) Find the cost of 2 cakes at 43p each, 4 bottles of lemonade at 24p each and 6 packets of crisps at 17p each.
6) How much is each person's share if £72.49 is shared equally between 11 people?
7) Mark bought 5 model cars at £1.87 each at a shop. What change should he have received if he gave the shopkeeper 2 £5 notes?
8) 8 people shared equally a £500 prize. How much did each person receive?
9) James earns £28.74 less each week than Fred. If Fred earns £142.12, how much does James earn?
10) Admission to the funfair was £1.25 for an adult and 75p for a child. Mr and Mrs Brown and their 3 children went to the funfair. How much did it cost them altogether?

A FRACTIONS

A fraction is a PART of a whole thing

e.g.   This pie is shared equally
       between 5 people

Each person gets $\frac{1}{5}$ of a pie
(1 pie divided by 5)

$\frac{1}{5}$ is a FRACTION

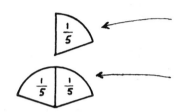

This FRACTION is $\frac{1}{5}$
(one fifth) of the pie

This FRACTION is $\frac{2}{5}$
(two fifths) of the pie , etc.

B WHAT SORT OF FRACTION? HOW MANY?

This shape is divided into
4 equal parts

e.g.

$\overline{4}$ ← DENOMINATOR
tells you what sort
of fraction

and 3 parts are
shaded

$\frac{3}{4}$ ← NUMERATOR
tells you how many

$\frac{3}{4}$ of the shape is shaded.

C A FRACTION IS A DIVISION

The line in the middle of a fraction means 'DIVIDED BY'

e.g.   (1)   7 divided by 8 can be written as a fraction $\frac{7}{8}$
e.g.   (2)   If 2 bars of chocolate are shared equally between
              3 people, each person gets $\frac{2}{3}$ of a bar of chocolate.
              (2 DIVIDED BY 3)

2 bars of chocolate

1 BAR OF CHOCOLATE	1 BAR OF CHOCOLATE

divided by 3

$\frac{1}{3}$	$\frac{1}{3}$	$\frac{1}{3}$	$\frac{1}{3}$	$\frac{1}{3}$	$\frac{1}{3}$

$\frac{2}{3}$ $\frac{2}{3}$ $\frac{2}{3}$

a

In each drawing, what fraction is shaded?

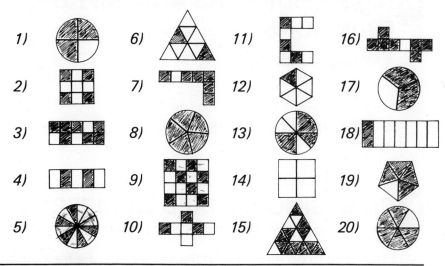

1) 2) 3) 4) 5) 6) 7) 8) 9) 10) 11) 12) 13) 14) 15) 16) 17) 18) 19) 20)

b

Write these divisions as fractions

1) 2 divided by 5
2) 5 divided by 8
3) 3 divided by 4
4) 7 divided by 12
5) 1 divided by 3
6) 4 divided by 7
7) 8 divided by 3
8) 13 divided by 20
9) 6 divided by 5
10) 9 divided by 10

c

1) One cake was shared equally by 4 boys. What fraction of the cake did each boy have?
2) Two equal plots of land were shared equally by 3 gardeners. What fraction of land did each gardener have?
3) An amount of money was divided equally between 6 people. What fraction did each have?
4) If 3 is divided by 5, what is the answer as a fraction?
5) 5 buns were shared equally between 6 girls. What fraction of a bun did each girl receive?
6) A path was 8 miles long. Bill walked 7 miles and then stopped. What fraction of the path had he walked along?
7) 2 tonnes of coal were put into 5 boxes so that the same amount of coal was in each box. What fraction of a tonne was in each box?
8) 1 week is divided equally into 7 days. What fraction of a week is each day?
9) A large window was divided into 10 equal small windows. 3 of the small windows had coloured glass in them. What fraction of the large window had coloured glass?
10) A soccer team has 11 players. In a certain team, 5 of the players were married. What fraction of the team was married?

A MIXED NUMBERS AND IMPROPER FRACTIONS

A **MIXED NUMBER** is a mixture of a whole number and a fraction

e.g. $3\frac{2}{3}$, $1\frac{3}{4}$

An **IMPROPER FRACTION** is a fraction with its top larger than its bottom

e.g. $\frac{25}{8}$, $\frac{7}{2}$

B CHANGING A MIXED NUMBER TO AN IMPROPER FRACTION

(You need to do this often at the beginning of a fraction problem)

e.g. $2\frac{3}{4}$

*1) Whole number times bottom $2 \times 4 = 8$
*2) Add the top $8 + 3 = 11$
*3) Put over the bottom $\frac{11}{4}$

C CHANGING A WHOLE NUMBER TO AN IMPROPER FRACTION

* Put it over 1   e.g. $3 = \frac{3}{1}$

     $7 = \frac{7}{1}$

D CHANGING AN IMPROPER FRACTION TO A MIXED NUMBER

(You need to do this often at the end of a fraction problem)

e.g. $\frac{13}{3}$

*1) Divide top by bottom $13 \div 3 = 4$ rem. 1
*2) Put remainder over bottom $4\frac{1}{3}$

IF THERE IS NO REMAINDER, JUST WRITE THE WHOLE NUMBER

e.g. $\frac{9}{1} = 9$, $\frac{4}{1} = 4$

a Change these to IMPROPER FRACTIONS

1) $3\frac{1}{3}$ 6) $4\frac{1}{2}$ 11) $2\frac{3}{8}$ 16) $3\frac{5}{6}$

2) $2\frac{1}{4}$ 7) 8 12) $6\frac{2}{3}$ 17) $7\frac{1}{7}$

3) $4\frac{2}{5}$ 8) $3\frac{4}{7}$ 13) 2 18) $2\frac{11}{12}$

4) $1\frac{3}{7}$ 9) $5\frac{9}{10}$ 14) $1\frac{1}{16}$ 19) 5

5) $2\frac{5}{6}$ 10) $1\frac{1}{2}$ 15) $4\frac{1}{4}$ 20) $1\frac{7}{8}$

b Write the following as improper fractions

1) $1\frac{7}{12}$ 6) $4\frac{3}{8}$ 11) $3\frac{3}{4}$ 16) $2\frac{3}{5}$

2) $3\frac{1}{6}$ 7) $10\frac{1}{3}$ 12) $2\frac{8}{9}$ 17) $1\frac{5}{11}$

3) $6\frac{2}{5}$ 8) $1\frac{6}{7}$ 13) $4\frac{7}{10}$ 18) 7

4) $5\frac{1}{2}$ 9) $1\frac{15}{16}$ 14) 12 19) $25\frac{1}{2}$

5) 3 10) $4\frac{1}{8}$ 15) $5\frac{2}{3}$ 20) $8\frac{1}{4}$

c Change these to MIXED NUMBERS (or whole numbers if there are no remainders)

1) $\frac{3}{2}$ 6) $\frac{23}{7}$ 11) $\frac{17}{4}$ 16) $\frac{21}{8}$

2) $\frac{4}{3}$ 7) $\frac{6}{1}$ 12) $\frac{43}{8}$ 17) $\frac{37}{10}$

3) $\frac{7}{4}$ 8) $\frac{7}{2}$ 13) $\frac{2}{1}$ 18) $\frac{54}{5}$

4) $\frac{10}{7}$ 9) $\frac{29}{6}$ 14) $\frac{20}{3}$ 19) $\frac{13}{6}$

5) $\frac{12}{5}$ 10) $\frac{8}{5}$ 15) $\frac{11}{6}$ 20) $\frac{11}{2}$

d Express the following as mixed numbers (or whole numbers)

1) $\frac{11}{3}$ 6) $\frac{8}{1}$ 11) $\frac{11}{4}$ 16) $\frac{19}{5}$

2) $\frac{33}{7}$ 7) $\frac{26}{3}$ 12) $\frac{17}{11}$ 17) $\frac{7}{3}$

3) $\frac{25}{4}$ 8) $\frac{15}{8}$ 13) $\frac{24}{1}$ 18) $\frac{16}{9}$

4) $\frac{9}{2}$ 9) $\frac{13}{10}$ 14) $\frac{9}{5}$ 19) $\frac{17}{16}$

5) $\frac{6}{5}$ 10) $\frac{100}{3}$ 15) $\frac{47}{2}$ 20) $\frac{23}{6}$

A CANCELLING to make a fraction simpler.

* Divide top AND bottom by the SAME NUMBER

e.g. (1) Cancel $\dfrac{18}{22}$

2 will divide into top and bottom

$$\dfrac{18 \div 2 = 9}{22 \div 2 = 11}$$

e.g. (2) Cancel $\dfrac{15}{35}$

5 will divide into top and bottom

$$\dfrac{15 \div 5 = 3}{35 \div 5 = 7}$$

B LOWEST TERMS

A fraction in its simplest form is called 'IN ITS LOWEST TERMS'

* To express a fraction in its LOWEST TERMS,
  cancel it until you are sure it will not cancel any more

ALWAYS CHOOSE THE LARGEST NUMBER YOU CAN
THINK OF WHICH WILL DIVIDE INTO TOP AND BOTTOM

e.g. $\dfrac{18}{60}$

2 will divide into top and bottom
and 3 will divide into top and bottom
and 6 will divide into top and bottom
so DIVIDE TOP AND BOTTOM BY 6

$$\dfrac{\cancel{18}^{\,3}}{\cancel{60}_{\,10}} = \dfrac{3}{10}$$

a

Divide top and bottom of each fraction by 2.

1) $\frac{6}{14}$ 3) $\frac{12}{18}$ 5) $\frac{22}{24}$ 7) $\frac{2}{18}$ 9) $\frac{20}{42}$

2) $\frac{2}{8}$ 4) $\frac{16}{26}$ 6) $\frac{4}{10}$ 8) $\frac{8}{34}$ 10) $\frac{4}{50}$

b

Divide top and bottom of each fraction by 3.

1) $\frac{9}{12}$ 3) $\frac{24}{30}$ 5) $\frac{3}{15}$ 7) $\frac{33}{36}$ 9) $\frac{12}{15}$

2) $\frac{18}{21}$ 4) $\frac{6}{9}$ 6) $\frac{6}{27}$ 8) $\frac{21}{30}$ 10) $\frac{3}{18}$

c

Cancel by 10 (Divide top and bottom of each fraction by 10)

1) $\frac{50}{90}$ 3) $\frac{150}{160}$ 5) $\frac{90}{100}$ 7) $\frac{60}{110}$ 9) $\frac{70}{1000}$

2) $\frac{40}{70}$ 4) $\frac{100}{130}$ 6) $\frac{10}{120}$ 8) $\frac{20}{50}$ 10) $\frac{30}{80}$

d

Cancel by 6

1) $\frac{6}{12}$ 3) $\frac{24}{30}$ 5) $\frac{18}{42}$ 7) $\frac{6}{60}$ 9) $\frac{66}{84}$

2) $\frac{42}{48}$ 4) $\frac{12}{54}$ 6) $\frac{36}{66}$ 8) $\frac{30}{72}$ 10) $\frac{18}{24}$

e

For each fraction, find a number which will divide into top AND bottom. Use the number you have found to express the fraction in its lowest terms.

1) $\frac{6}{15}$ 6) $\frac{3}{12}$ 11) $\frac{16}{40}$ 16) $\frac{27}{36}$

2) $\frac{10}{25}$ 7) $\frac{8}{12}$ 12) $\frac{15}{55}$ 17) $\frac{50}{100}$

3) $\frac{2}{12}$ 8) $\frac{18}{20}$ 13) $\frac{21}{27}$ 18) $\frac{54}{90}$

4) $\frac{50}{80}$ 9) $\frac{4}{20}$ 14) $\frac{88}{99}$ 19) $\frac{6}{36}$

5) $\frac{12}{18}$ 10) $\frac{21}{28}$ 15) $\frac{4}{6}$ 20) $\frac{36}{60}$

Have you cancelled all these as far as they will go?
Are they all in their lowest terms?

A CANCELLING WITH A **X** SIGN

* Divide ONE TOP and ONE BOTTOM by the same number

e.g. (1)

$$\frac{6}{11} \times \frac{5}{9}$$

$$\frac{6}{11} \times \frac{5}{9}$$

Both 6 and 9 will divide by 3

$$\frac{2\,\cancel{6}}{11} \times \frac{5}{\cancel{9}\,3}$$

$$\frac{2}{11} \times \frac{5}{3}$$

---

e.g. (2)

$$\frac{4}{15} \times \frac{5}{7} \times \frac{11}{16}$$

$$\frac{4}{15} \times \frac{5}{7} \times \frac{11}{16}$$

Both 4 and 16 will divide by 4

$$\frac{\cancel{4}^{1}}{15} \times \frac{5}{7} \times \frac{11}{\cancel{16}\,4}$$

$$\frac{1}{15} \times \frac{5}{7} \times \frac{11}{4}$$

Both 15 and 5 will divide by 5

$$\frac{1}{_3\cancel{15}} \times \frac{\cancel{5}^{1}}{7} \times \frac{11}{4}$$

$$\frac{1}{3} \times \frac{1}{7} \times \frac{11}{4}$$

a

Cancel these groups of fractions

1) $\frac{1}{3} \times \frac{3}{4}$ 6) $\frac{5}{6} \times \frac{1}{15}$ 11) $\frac{6}{5} \times \frac{7}{10}$

2) $\frac{2}{3} \times \frac{1}{2}$ 7) $\frac{7}{12} \times \frac{6}{5}$ 12) $\frac{3}{5} \times \frac{7}{12}$

3) $\frac{3}{7} \times \frac{2}{3}$ 8) $\frac{3}{4} \times \frac{16}{25}$ 13) $\frac{7}{8} \times \frac{8}{9}$

4) $\frac{2}{3} \times \frac{1}{4}$ 9) $\frac{6}{13} \times \frac{1}{9}$ 14) $\frac{7}{10} \times \frac{20}{23}$

5) $\frac{5}{6} \times \frac{3}{4}$ 10) $\frac{10}{7} \times \frac{2}{5}$ 15) $\frac{24}{25} \times \frac{1}{4}$

b

Cancel these groups of fractions

1) $\frac{2}{3} \times \frac{3}{4}$ 6) $\frac{11}{15} \times \frac{7}{11}$ 11) $\frac{6}{35} \times \frac{7}{12}$

2) $\frac{1}{5} \times \frac{15}{16}$ 7) $\frac{3}{10} \times \frac{5}{21}$ 12) $\frac{10}{11} \times \frac{5}{4}$

3) $\frac{5}{3} \times \frac{3}{5}$ 8) $\frac{16}{7} \times \frac{7}{8}$ 13) $\frac{12}{25} \times \frac{5}{16}$

4) $\frac{7}{8} \times \frac{5}{14}$ 9) $\frac{2}{5} \times \frac{25}{4}$ 14) $\frac{20}{21} \times \frac{7}{8}$

5) $\frac{4}{5} \times \frac{15}{16}$ 10) $\frac{7}{18} \times \frac{2}{3}$ 15) $\frac{13}{6} \times \frac{15}{26}$

c

Cancel these groups of fractions

1) $\frac{1}{4} \times \frac{4}{3} \times \frac{1}{5}$ 6) $\frac{1}{3} \times \frac{2}{5} \times \frac{5}{8}$ 11) $\frac{25}{4} \times \frac{16}{1} \times \frac{11}{15}$

2) $\frac{7}{8} \times \frac{3}{5} \times \frac{10}{11}$ 7) $\frac{3}{8} \times \frac{10}{7} \times \frac{14}{9}$ 12) $\frac{8}{39} \times \frac{13}{24}$

3) $\frac{12}{15} \times \frac{11}{18}$ 8) $\frac{11}{12} \times \frac{3}{8} \times \frac{5}{22}$ 13) $\frac{5}{2} \times \frac{4}{7} \times \frac{7}{2}$

4) $\frac{5}{6} \times \frac{1}{7} \times \frac{12}{13}$ 9) $\frac{4}{5} \times \frac{1}{9} \times \frac{1}{10}$ 14) $\frac{15}{28} \times \frac{7}{16} \times \frac{8}{25}$

5) $\frac{10}{3} \times \frac{1}{4} \times \frac{8}{15}$ 10) $\frac{5}{6} \times \frac{7}{13} \times \frac{9}{20}$ 15) $\frac{6}{1} \times \frac{1}{5} \times \frac{17}{18}$

d

Cancel these groups of fractions. Write any whole numbers as fractions, e.g. write 2 as $\frac{2}{1}$, 5 as $\frac{5}{1}$, etc.

1) $\frac{3}{8} \times \frac{4}{5} \times \frac{1}{3}$ 6) $\frac{11}{12} \times \frac{3}{7} \times \frac{35}{26} \times \frac{13}{44}$ 11) $\frac{15}{16} \times \frac{5}{48}$

2) $2 \times \frac{7}{8}$ 7) $5 \times \frac{9}{65}$ 12) $\frac{9}{8} \times 7 \times \frac{32}{35}$

3) $\frac{2}{3} \times 3$ 8) $\frac{18}{31} \times \frac{31}{48}$ 13) $10 \times \frac{9}{14} \times \frac{7}{25}$

4) $\frac{3}{4} \times \frac{10}{11} \times \frac{8}{9}$ 9) $\frac{10}{21} \times \frac{14}{25} \times 6$ 14) $\frac{6}{11} \times 4 \times \frac{22}{45}$

5) $\frac{11}{17} \times \frac{51}{55}$ 10) $\frac{4}{5} \times \frac{5}{6} \times \frac{5}{8}$ 15) $\frac{35}{18} \times \frac{9}{10} \times \frac{4}{7}$

A LOWEST COMMON DENOMINATOR (LCD)

(The bottom of a fraction is called the DENOMINATOR)
* To find the lowest common denominator, look for the
  lowest number that ALL THE DENOMINATORS WILL DIVIDE INTO

e.g. (1) $\qquad \dfrac{1}{4} , \dfrac{2}{3} , \dfrac{1}{2}$

4 will divide into 12
3 will divide into 12
2 will divide into 12
They will not divide into anything smaller,
so 12 is the LCD

$$\dfrac{}{12} , \dfrac{}{12} , \dfrac{}{12}$$

---

e.g. (2) $\qquad \dfrac{5}{8} + \dfrac{3}{4}$

8 will divide into 8
4 will divide into 8
so 8 is the LCD

$$\dfrac{}{8} + \dfrac{}{8}$$

HINTS

(THESE MAY HELP BUT THEY DO NOT ALWAYS GIVE THE
CORRECT LCD)

1) Look at the larger (or largest) denominator.
   Is this the LCD?
   $$\dfrac{3}{4} , \dfrac{5}{12}$$

Yes. 12 is the LCD $\qquad \dfrac{}{12} , \dfrac{}{12}$

2) If this will not work, try multiplying the denominators.
   Does this give the LCD? $\dfrac{2}{3} , \dfrac{1}{5}$

Yes. 3 x 5 = 15 $\qquad$ so 15 is the LCD $\qquad \dfrac{}{15} , \dfrac{}{15}$

a Find the LOWEST COMMON DENOMINATOR of each group of fractions (Pretend the tops of the fractions are not there)

1) $\frac{2}{3}$, $\frac{1}{2}$ 6) $\frac{1}{2}$, $\frac{3}{5}$ 11) $\frac{5}{1}$, $\frac{7}{9}$

2) $\frac{1}{2}$, $\frac{3}{4}$ 7) $\frac{5}{6}$, $\frac{7}{12}$ 12) $\frac{3}{10}$, $\frac{1}{2}$

3) $\frac{3}{5}$, $\frac{7}{10}$ 8) $\frac{3}{4}$, $\frac{5}{8}$ 13) $\frac{3}{2}$, $\frac{1}{6}$

4) $\frac{1}{4}$, $\frac{2}{3}$ 9) $\frac{3}{5}$, $\frac{3}{4}$ 14) $\frac{7}{4}$, $\frac{3}{1}$

5) $\frac{4}{5}$, $\frac{1}{3}$ 10) $\frac{8}{3}$, $\frac{5}{6}$ 15) $\frac{11}{6}$, $\frac{7}{5}$

b Find the LCD of each group (Pretend the tops of the fractions are not there)

1) $\frac{5}{2}$, $\frac{5}{8}$ 6) $\frac{22}{7}$, $\frac{1}{2}$ 11) $\frac{3}{1}$, $\frac{11}{12}$

2) $\frac{9}{10}$, $\frac{13}{4}$ 7) $\frac{10}{3}$, $\frac{7}{1}$ 12) $\frac{2}{5}$, $\frac{4}{7}$

3) $\frac{5}{8}$, $\frac{1}{3}$ 8) $\frac{1}{6}$, $\frac{9}{2}$ 13) $\frac{5}{6}$, $\frac{5}{9}$

4) $\frac{1}{8}$, $\frac{2}{5}$ 9) $\frac{6}{5}$, $\frac{1}{5}$ 14) $\frac{2}{3}$, $\frac{11}{16}$

5) $\frac{17}{6}$, $\frac{5}{4}$ 10) $\frac{21}{4}$, $\frac{5}{12}$ 15) $\frac{8}{9}$, $\frac{1}{2}$

c Find the LCD of each group (Pretend the tops of the fractions are not there)

1) $\frac{1}{2}$, $\frac{1}{4}$, $\frac{1}{8}$ 6) $\frac{5}{8}$, $\frac{3}{4}$, $\frac{2}{3}$ 11) $\frac{6}{7}$, $\frac{4}{5}$

2) $\frac{3}{4}$, $\frac{2}{3}$, $\frac{1}{2}$ 7) $\frac{4}{3}$, $\frac{15}{2}$, $\frac{7}{6}$ 12) $\frac{2}{1}$, $\frac{5}{2}$, $\frac{9}{4}$

3) $\frac{7}{8}$, $\frac{5}{2}$, $\frac{1}{8}$ 8) $\frac{17}{10}$, $\frac{8}{5}$, $\frac{1}{2}$ 13) $\frac{13}{15}$, $\frac{9}{10}$, $\frac{23}{6}$

4) $\frac{5}{3}$, $\frac{6}{7}$ 9) $\frac{3}{8}$, $\frac{19}{6}$ 14) $\frac{1}{4}$, $\frac{1}{5}$, $\frac{1}{6}$

5) $\frac{23}{3}$, $\frac{11}{6}$, $\frac{5}{4}$ 10) $\frac{1}{8}$, $\frac{3}{1}$, $\frac{7}{4}$ 15) $\frac{1}{2}$, $\frac{1}{6}$, $\frac{1}{3}$, $\frac{1}{4}$

d Find the LCD of each group of fractions (Pretend the tops of the fractions and the + and − signs are not there)

1) $\frac{5}{6}$ + $\frac{7}{4}$ 6) $\frac{8}{5}$ − $\frac{4}{3}$ 11) $\frac{5}{2}$ + $\frac{2}{5}$ + $\frac{3}{4}$

2) $\frac{2}{3}$ + $\frac{3}{4}$ 7) $\frac{1}{7}$ + $\frac{3}{4}$ 12) $\frac{7}{6}$ + $\frac{3}{4}$ + $\frac{9}{8}$

3) $\frac{7}{10}$ − $\frac{4}{25}$ 8) $\frac{1}{2}$ − $\frac{3}{10}$ 13) $\frac{4}{1}$ − $\frac{6}{5}$ − $\frac{11}{10}$

4) $\frac{5}{6}$ + $\frac{1}{3}$ 9) $\frac{19}{10}$ − $\frac{5}{3}$ 14) $\frac{8}{5}$ + $\frac{13}{10}$ − $\frac{7}{6}$

5) $\frac{7}{8}$ − $\frac{1}{2}$ 10) $\frac{11}{4}$ + $\frac{3}{20}$ 15) $\frac{4}{5}$ − $\frac{2}{7}$ + $\frac{3}{2}$

A+ ADDITION

e.g. $3\frac{3}{4} + 1\frac{2}{3}$

*1) If there are any WHOLE NUMBERS, add them first and keep till the end

$4 \quad \frac{3}{4} + \frac{2}{3}$

*2) Find LOWEST COMMON DENOMINATOR

$4 \quad \frac{}{12} + \frac{}{12}$

*3) Put in new tops (numerators)

$\frac{3}{4}$

$12 \div 4 = 3$

$3 \times 3 = 9$

$\frac{2}{3}$

$12 \div 3 = 4$

$4 \times 2 = 8$

$4 \quad \frac{9}{12} + \frac{8}{12}$

*4) Add tops
DO NOT CHANGE BOTTOMS

$4 \quad \frac{17}{12}$

*5) If the fraction is improper, change to mixed numbers

$4 \qquad 1\frac{5}{12}$

*6) Add on any whole numbers

$4 + 1\frac{5}{12} = 5\frac{5}{12}$

---

e.g. (2) $\quad 2\frac{3}{5} + \frac{7}{10} + 3\frac{3}{4}$

$2 + 3 = 5$

$5 \quad \frac{3}{5} + \frac{7}{10} + \frac{3}{4}$

$5 \quad \frac{12}{20} + \frac{14}{20} + \frac{15}{20}$

$5 \quad \frac{41}{20}$

$5 \qquad 2\frac{1}{20}$

$7\frac{1}{20}$

e.g. (3)

$\frac{5}{6} + \frac{1}{3}$

$\frac{5}{6} + \frac{2}{6}$

$\frac{7}{6}$

$1\frac{1}{6}$

NEVER ADD BOTTOMS

a

1) $\frac{1}{2} + \frac{1}{3}$ 6) $2\frac{1}{6} + \frac{3}{4}$ 11) $2\frac{4}{5} + 1\frac{1}{2}$ 16) $3\frac{1}{2} + 4\frac{3}{4}$

2) $\frac{1}{4} + \frac{1}{2}$ 7) $2\frac{2}{3} + 1\frac{1}{2}$ 12) $1\frac{1}{2} + 1\frac{5}{6}$ 17) $\frac{7}{10} + 1\frac{1}{2}$

3) $\frac{2}{3} + \frac{3}{4}$ 8) $\frac{4}{9} + \frac{1}{3}$ 13) $\frac{3}{4} + 4\frac{1}{8}$ 18) $\frac{3}{4} + \frac{1}{5}$

4) $\frac{1}{2} + \frac{1}{7}$ 9) $1\frac{1}{3} + 1\frac{1}{4}$ 14) $\frac{2}{5} + \frac{3}{10}$ 19) $2\frac{5}{6} + \frac{2}{3}$

5) $\frac{1}{5} + \frac{3}{5}$ 10) $4 + \frac{3}{8}$ 15) $2\frac{3}{8} + 1\frac{5}{8}$ 20) $3\frac{2}{3} + 1\frac{3}{5}$

b

1) $1\frac{2}{3} + 2\frac{2}{3}$ 6) $5\frac{2}{5} + 1\frac{3}{4}$ 11) $3\frac{1}{4} + 6\frac{2}{3}$ 16) $\frac{3}{7} + \frac{1}{3}$

2) $3\frac{7}{12} + 1\frac{1}{2}$ 7) $\frac{3}{5} + 2$ 12) $4 + 1\frac{9}{10}$ 17) $1\frac{3}{8} + 2\frac{7}{8}$

3) $2\frac{3}{4} + 4\frac{1}{2}$ 8) $2\frac{2}{3} + 5\frac{1}{2}$ 13) $\frac{5}{9} + \frac{5}{6}$ 18) $3\frac{4}{5} + \frac{1}{3}$

4) $\frac{3}{8} + \frac{2}{3}$ 9) $2\frac{1}{6} + 3\frac{5}{8}$ 14) $\frac{7}{10} + 3\frac{1}{4}$ 19) $5\frac{3}{5} + 2\frac{1}{2}$

5) $1\frac{3}{4} + 4\frac{7}{8}$ 10) $\frac{7}{8} + \frac{5}{16}$ 15) $2\frac{3}{4} + \frac{5}{6}$ 20) $3\frac{3}{8} + 2\frac{2}{5}$

c

Find the sum of each of these groups of numbers

1) $3\frac{3}{4}$, $8\frac{5}{8}$ 6) $3\frac{11}{16}$, $2\frac{1}{4}$ 11) $\frac{1}{2}$, $\frac{1}{3}$, $\frac{1}{4}$

2) $7\frac{5}{6}$, $1\frac{1}{2}$ 7) $5\frac{5}{6}$, $\frac{3}{4}$ 12) $\frac{7}{8}$, $\frac{3}{4}$, $\frac{5}{6}$

3) $5\frac{1}{5}$, $2\frac{1}{4}$ 8) $1\frac{3}{4}$, $2\frac{5}{9}$ 13) $1\frac{2}{3}$, $2\frac{1}{6}$, $\frac{1}{2}$

4) $\frac{1}{6}$, $\frac{3}{5}$ 9) $5\frac{7}{13}$, $1\frac{8}{13}$ 14) $3\frac{1}{2}$, $1\frac{1}{4}$, $2\frac{5}{8}$

5) $\frac{9}{10}$, $3\frac{2}{5}$ 10) $12\frac{2}{3}$, $2\frac{4}{5}$ 15) $\frac{3}{5}$, $1\frac{7}{10}$, $\frac{1}{4}$

d

1) $\frac{6}{7} + \frac{3}{7} + \frac{2}{7}$

2) $2\frac{5}{8} + 5\frac{7}{12}$

3) $\frac{2}{3} + \frac{3}{4} + \frac{4}{5}$

4) $\frac{5}{6} + 2\frac{11}{16}$

5) $\frac{1}{6} + \frac{1}{3} + \frac{3}{4} + \frac{1}{2}$

6) $2\frac{1}{4} + 8\frac{1}{6}$

7) $16\frac{3}{5} + 19\frac{2}{3}$

8) $1\frac{9}{10} + \frac{1}{2} + 6\frac{4}{5}$

9) Find the sum of $3\frac{7}{12}$ and $2\frac{1}{9}$

10) Find the sum of $6\frac{1}{8}$, $4\frac{3}{5}$ and $\frac{1}{4}$

11) Find the sum of $1\frac{5}{6}$, $2\frac{5}{9}$ and $3\frac{1}{3}$

12) Find the sum of $8\frac{1}{4}$ and $7\frac{3}{5}$

13) Find the sum of $13\frac{2}{5}$, $11\frac{1}{3}$ and $8\frac{3}{10}$

14) Find the sum of $\frac{1}{4}$, $\frac{1}{6}$, $\frac{1}{12}$ and $\frac{1}{9}$

15) Find the sum of $2\frac{2}{9}$ and $1\frac{3}{8}$

A — **SUBTRACTION**

e.g. $4\frac{1}{3} - 1\frac{4}{5}$

*1) If there are any WHOLE NUMBERS, subtract them first and keep till the end

$3 \quad \frac{1}{3} - \frac{4}{5}$

*2) Find LOWEST COMMON DENOMINATOR

$3 \dfrac{}{15} - \dfrac{}{15}$

*3) Put in new tops (numerators)

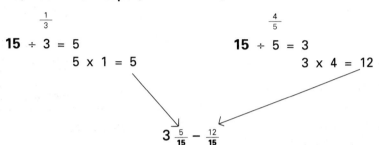

$\frac{1}{3}$

$15 \div 3 = 5$

$\qquad 5 \times 1 = 5$

$\frac{4}{5}$

$15 \div 5 = 3$

$\qquad 3 \times 4 = 12$

$3\frac{5}{15} - \frac{12}{15}$

*4) If left top is smaller than right top, borrow a whole one from the whole number

$3 \qquad \frac{5}{15} - \frac{12}{15}$

$2\frac{15}{15} + \frac{5}{15} - \frac{12}{15}$

*5) Work out tops
DO NOT CHANGE BOTTOMS

$2\frac{8}{15}$

---

e.g. (2)

$3\frac{1}{5} - 1\frac{3}{4}$

$2 \quad \frac{1}{5} - \frac{3}{4}$

$2 \dfrac{}{20} - \dfrac{}{20}$

$2 \frac{4}{20} - \frac{15}{20}$

$1\frac{20}{20} + \frac{4}{20} - \frac{15}{20}$

$1\frac{9}{20}$

e.g. (3)

$5\frac{7}{8} - 1\frac{1}{2}$

$4 \quad \frac{7}{8} - \frac{1}{2}$

$4 \dfrac{}{8} - \dfrac{}{8}$

$4 \frac{7}{8} - \frac{4}{8}$

$4\frac{3}{8}$

NEVER SUBTRACT BOTTOMS

a

1) $\frac{4}{5} - \frac{3}{5}$ 6) $\frac{3}{4} - \frac{1}{2}$ 11) $\frac{7}{12} - \frac{1}{2}$ 16) $3\frac{1}{6} - \frac{3}{4}$

2) $\frac{6}{7} - \frac{2}{7}$ 7) $\frac{2}{3} - \frac{1}{2}$ 12) $\frac{11}{15} - \frac{4}{15}$ 17) $3\frac{1}{2} - 1\frac{1}{4}$

3) $\frac{7}{9} - \frac{5}{9}$ 8) $\frac{7}{8} - \frac{1}{4}$ 13) $1\frac{1}{3} - \frac{1}{2}$ 18) $4\frac{3}{10} - 2\frac{1}{2}$

4) $\frac{2}{3} - \frac{1}{3}$ 9) $\frac{5}{6} - \frac{2}{3}$ 14) $2\frac{1}{4} - \frac{2}{3}$ 19) $3\frac{3}{4} - 1\frac{1}{8}$

5) $\frac{9}{11} - \frac{3}{11}$ 10) $\frac{9}{10} - \frac{3}{5}$ 15) $1\frac{5}{8} - \frac{1}{2}$ 20) $2\frac{1}{5} - \frac{1}{4}$

b

1) $2\frac{2}{3} - \frac{3}{4}$ 6) $3\frac{3}{8} - \frac{3}{4}$ 11) $5\frac{1}{9} - 4\frac{2}{3}$ 16) $\frac{1}{4} - \frac{1}{9}$

2) $1\frac{1}{6} - \frac{1}{2}$ 7) $3\frac{1}{3} - \frac{2}{3}$ 12) $2\frac{4}{5} - \frac{1}{10}$ 17) $5\frac{1}{2} - 3\frac{2}{3}$

3) $\frac{7}{12} - \frac{3}{8}$ 8) $5\frac{1}{5} - \frac{3}{4}$ 13) $6\frac{1}{2} - 1\frac{3}{4}$ 18) $3\frac{1}{6} - 1\frac{2}{5}$

4) $2\frac{1}{2} - \frac{1}{3}$ 9) $3\frac{1}{4} - \frac{5}{6}$ 14) $1\frac{3}{4} - \frac{11}{12}$ 19) $3\frac{1}{3} - 3\frac{1}{5}$

5) $2\frac{2}{5} - 1\frac{2}{3}$ 10) $4\frac{1}{2} - 1\frac{3}{5}$ 15) $2\frac{1}{6} - \frac{5}{9}$ 20) $2\frac{3}{8} - \frac{5}{6}$

c

If necessary, write whole numbers as fractions,
e.g. write 4 as $\frac{4}{1}$, 7 as $\frac{7}{1}$, etc.

1) $1\frac{3}{5} - 1\frac{1}{2}$ 6) $4\frac{1}{4} - \frac{3}{5}$ 11) $\frac{5}{6} - \frac{11}{16}$ 16) $4\frac{2}{3} - 1$

2) $2\frac{1}{4} - \frac{9}{10}$ 7) $3 - \frac{5}{8}$ 12) $2\frac{1}{8} - \frac{5}{8}$ 17) $1\frac{5}{16} - \frac{3}{4}$

3) $\frac{1}{2} - \frac{2}{7}$ 8) $\frac{11}{15} - \frac{2}{5}$ 13) $5 - \frac{5}{6}$ 18) $2\frac{1}{10} - \frac{1}{5}$

4) $3\frac{2}{3} - \frac{1}{4}$ 9) $8\frac{1}{2} - 2\frac{2}{3}$ 14) $1\frac{1}{7} - \frac{4}{5}$ 19) $1\frac{5}{6} - \frac{4}{9}$

5) $5\frac{4}{5} - 1\frac{1}{5}$ 10) $1\frac{5}{6} - \frac{7}{10}$ 15) $2\frac{5}{12} - \frac{5}{8}$ 20) $\frac{13}{16} - \frac{7}{12}$

d

1) $2\frac{1}{3} - \frac{5}{8}$

2) $1\frac{1}{2} - \frac{3}{11}$

3) $2\frac{1}{6} - 1\frac{3}{4}$

4) $6 - 1\frac{1}{4}$

5) $2\frac{3}{7} - \frac{6}{7}$

6) $\frac{11}{20} - \frac{11}{24}$

7) $2\frac{3}{10} - \frac{1}{4}$

8) $2\frac{1}{2} - 1\frac{7}{9}$

9) $1\frac{1}{9} - \frac{7}{12}$

10) $4 - \frac{5}{12}$

11) From $3\frac{1}{4}$ subtract $2\frac{1}{2}$

12) From $2\frac{1}{3}$ subtract $\frac{8}{9}$

13) From $6\frac{1}{2}$ subtract $1\frac{4}{5}$

14) From 10 subtract $2\frac{2}{3}$

15) Find the difference between $4\frac{5}{6}$ and $4\frac{1}{4}$

16) Find the difference between $3\frac{1}{3}$ and $\frac{5}{7}$

17) Find the difference between $2\frac{1}{8}$ and $\frac{7}{16}$

18) Subtract $\frac{10}{11}$ from $1\frac{1}{3}$

19) Subtract $\frac{5}{6}$ from $2\frac{1}{9}$

20) Subtract $\frac{1}{6}$ from $3\frac{2}{3}$

A ➕➖ ADDITION & SUBTRACTION

Before you do these, make sure you have studied
pages 34 and 36.

e.g. $2\frac{1}{4} + \frac{5}{8} - 1\frac{1}{2}$

***1) If there are any WHOLE
NUMBERS, add or subtract first
and keep till the end**

$1 \quad \frac{1}{4} + \frac{5}{8} - \frac{1}{2}$

***2) Find LOWEST COMMON
DENOMINATOR**

$1 \quad \frac{}{8} + \frac{}{8} - \frac{}{8}$

*3) Put in new tops (numerators)

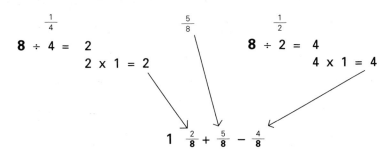

$\frac{1}{4}$ $\qquad$ $\frac{5}{8}$ $\qquad$ $\frac{1}{2}$

$8 \div 4 = 2 \qquad\qquad\qquad 8 \div 2 = 4$

$2 \times 1 = 2 \qquad\qquad\qquad 4 \times 1 = 4$

$1 \quad \frac{2}{8} + \frac{5}{8} - \frac{4}{8}$

***4) Add or subtract tops
DO NOT CHANGE BOTTOMS**

$1\frac{3}{8}$

---

e.g. (2)

$4\frac{1}{5} - 1\frac{3}{4} + \frac{3}{10}$

$3 \qquad \frac{1}{5} - \frac{3}{4} + \frac{3}{10}$

$3 \qquad \frac{4}{20} - \frac{15}{20} + \frac{6}{20}$

$2\frac{20}{20} + \qquad \frac{4}{20} - \frac{15}{20} + \frac{6}{20}$

$2 \quad \frac{\cancel{15}^{\,3}}{\cancel{20}_{\,4}}$

$2\frac{3}{4}$

e.g. (3)

$2\frac{2}{3} + 3\frac{3}{4} - 1\frac{1}{6}$

$4 \qquad \frac{2}{3} + \frac{3}{4} - \frac{1}{6}$

$4 \qquad \frac{8}{12} + \frac{9}{12} - \frac{2}{12}$

$4 \quad \frac{\cancel{15}^{\,5}}{\cancel{12}_{\,4}}$

$4 \quad \frac{5}{4}$

$5\frac{1}{4}$

NEVER ADD OR SUBTRACT BOTTOMS

a

1) $\frac{7}{8} + \frac{2}{3}$

2) $\frac{1}{3} + 1\frac{3}{5}$

3) $2\frac{3}{4} - \frac{5}{8}$

4) $\frac{8}{9} + 1\frac{1}{3}$

5) $3\frac{1}{2} - 1\frac{5}{6}$

6) $1\frac{1}{6} - \frac{2}{9}$

7) $6\frac{3}{4} + 2\frac{1}{2}$

8) $\frac{5}{8} - \frac{3}{5}$

9) $2\frac{2}{5} - \frac{9}{10}$

10) $\frac{1}{2} + 2\frac{1}{9}$

11) $4\frac{1}{4} - \frac{2}{3}$

12) $3 - 1\frac{1}{7}$

13) $2\frac{7}{12} + 1\frac{5}{9}$

14) $4\frac{1}{2} + 1\frac{2}{5}$

15) $\frac{5}{6} - \frac{11}{15}$

b

1) $3\frac{1}{6} - \frac{3}{4}$

2) $7\frac{5}{16} + 3\frac{3}{8}$

3) $6 - 3\frac{1}{8}$

4) $2\frac{3}{10} - \frac{1}{3}$

5) $2\frac{15}{16} + 1\frac{1}{12}$

6) Find the sum of $2\frac{3}{7}$ and $7\frac{2}{3}$

7) From $1\frac{1}{5}$ subtract $\frac{2}{3}$

8) Find the difference between $2\frac{1}{4}$ and $1\frac{1}{5}$

9) What is the sum of $3\frac{5}{6}$ and $4\frac{3}{8}$?

10) Subtract $\frac{5}{8}$ from $3\frac{1}{4}$

c

1) $1\frac{3}{4} + 2\frac{1}{2} + \frac{3}{8}$

2) $\frac{3}{4} + \frac{2}{3} - \frac{5}{6}$

3) $2\frac{1}{2} - \frac{3}{4} - \frac{7}{16}$

4) $3\frac{2}{3} + \frac{1}{6} - 1\frac{3}{4}$

5) $2\frac{7}{10} - 1\frac{1}{4} - \frac{3}{5}$

6) $\frac{8}{9} + 2\frac{1}{3} - 1\frac{5}{6}$

7) $\frac{3}{5} + \frac{5}{6} - \frac{1}{10}$

8) $1\frac{3}{4} + 1\frac{3}{5} - \frac{1}{2}$

9) $2\frac{3}{5} - 1\frac{3}{10} + \frac{1}{2}$

10) $1\frac{5}{9} + \frac{1}{4} - \frac{5}{6}$

d

1) Find the sum of $1\frac{2}{3}$, $2\frac{3}{4}$ and $3\frac{4}{5}$

2) From the sum of $3\frac{2}{3}$ and $1\frac{1}{2}$ subtract $2\frac{5}{6}$

3) Subtract $4\frac{1}{2}$ from the sum of $2\frac{7}{8}$ and $1\frac{3}{4}$

4) Find the difference between $1\frac{1}{7}$ and $\frac{3}{4}$

5) From the sum of $1\frac{1}{4}$ and $2\frac{2}{3}$ subtract $\frac{7}{12}$

6) Add $3\frac{4}{5}$ to the difference between $2\frac{1}{10}$ and $\frac{1}{2}$

7) Subtract $\frac{5}{8}$ from the sum of $\frac{2}{3}$ and $\frac{1}{6}$

8) Add $2\frac{3}{10}$ to the sum of $3\frac{2}{5}$ and $1\frac{2}{3}$

9) From the sum of $2\frac{1}{2}$ and $1\frac{1}{3}$ subtract $3\frac{4}{9}$

10) Subtract $1\frac{9}{10}$ from the difference between $3\frac{1}{2}$ and $\frac{3}{5}$

A ✕ MULTIPLICATION

e.g. $\frac{2}{5} \times 3\frac{3}{4}$

*1) Turn any mixed numbers to IMPROPER fractions

$\frac{2}{5} \times \frac{15}{4}$

*2) CANCEL if you can

$\frac{\overset{1}{2}}{\underset{1}{5}} \times \frac{\overset{3}{15}}{\underset{2}{4}}$

*3) Multiply (TOPS ✕ TOPS, BOTTOMS ✕ BOTTOMS)

$\frac{1}{1} \times \frac{3}{2} = \frac{3}{2}$

*4) If improper, change to mixed numbers

$1\frac{1}{2}$

---

e.g. (2)

$1\frac{5}{9} \times \frac{3}{20} \times 3\frac{4}{7}$

$\frac{14}{9} \times \frac{3}{20} \times \frac{25}{7}$

$\frac{\overset{2}{14}}{\underset{3}{9}} \times \frac{\overset{1}{3}}{\underset{2}{20}} \times \frac{\overset{5}{25}}{\underset{1}{7}}$

$\frac{5}{6}$

e.g. (3)

$1\frac{1}{6} \times 2\frac{2}{3}$

$\frac{7}{6} \times \frac{8}{3}$

$\frac{7}{\underset{3}{6}} \times \frac{\overset{4}{8}}{3}$

$\frac{28}{9}$

$3\frac{1}{9}$

B OF means 'multiplied by'

e.g.

$\frac{7}{16}$ of $4\frac{4}{5}$

$\frac{7}{16} \times 4\frac{4}{5}$

$\frac{7}{16} \times \frac{24}{5}$

$\frac{7}{\underset{2}{16}} \times \frac{\overset{3}{24}}{5}$

$\frac{21}{10}$

$2\frac{1}{10}$

e.g

$\frac{1}{9}$ of $\frac{3}{4}$ of 54

$\frac{1}{9} \times \frac{3}{4} \times \frac{54}{1}$

$\frac{1}{\underset{1}{9}} \times \frac{3}{\underset{2}{4}} \times \frac{\overset{3}{54}}{1}$

$\frac{9}{2}$

$4\frac{1}{2}$

a

1) $\frac{1}{4} \times \frac{1}{2}$ 6) $1\frac{1}{3} \times \frac{1}{4}$ 11) $\frac{5}{7} \times 1\frac{3}{4}$ 16) $\frac{7}{8} \times \frac{4}{5}$

2) $\frac{2}{3} \times \frac{1}{5}$ 7) $4\frac{2}{5} \times \frac{3}{11}$ 12) $1\frac{1}{2} \times \frac{5}{8}$ 17) $1\frac{1}{4} \times 3\frac{3}{5}$

3) $\frac{3}{4} \times \frac{5}{8}$ 8) $1\frac{3}{7} \times 2\frac{4}{5}$ 13) $3\frac{3}{8} \times 1\frac{1}{3}$ 18) $2\frac{2}{5} \times 1\frac{1}{9}$

4) $\frac{3}{8} \times \frac{4}{5}$ 9) $1\frac{1}{5} \times \frac{7}{12}$ 14) $2\frac{1}{2} \times 2\frac{1}{2}$ 19) $2\frac{3}{4} \times 1\frac{1}{3}$

5) $\frac{2}{7} \times \frac{1}{6}$ 10) $\frac{2}{9} \times \frac{3}{4}$ 15) $\frac{9}{10} \times \frac{2}{3}$ 20) $\frac{7}{10} \times 2\frac{1}{2}$

---

b

Write any whole numbers as fractions,
e.g. Write 8 as $\frac{8}{1}$, 13 as $\frac{13}{1}$, etc.

1) $2\frac{1}{3} \times 2\frac{1}{4}$ 6) $\frac{5}{8} \times 7$ 11) $\frac{4}{5} \times \frac{5}{6} \times \frac{2}{3}$

2) $1\frac{3}{7} \times 2\frac{5}{8}$ 7) $\frac{3}{4}$ of $\frac{1}{6}$ 12) $1\frac{1}{3} \times \frac{9}{10} \times 1\frac{1}{4}$

3) $6 \times 1\frac{1}{4}$ 8) $\frac{2}{7} \times 8\frac{3}{4}$ 13) $\frac{1}{5}$ of $\frac{3}{4}$ of 1000

4) $2\frac{7}{10} \times 1\frac{5}{9}$ 9) $1\frac{1}{11} \times 3\frac{1}{7}$ 14) $1\frac{1}{4} \times 8 \times \frac{7}{15}$

5) $2\frac{1}{2} \times \frac{2}{5}$ 10) $\frac{7}{8}$ of 12   15) $\frac{3}{4}$ of $\frac{2}{3}$ of 84

---

c

1) $3\frac{1}{9} \times 5\frac{1}{4}$ 6) $\frac{1}{11} \times 6\frac{3}{5}$ 11) $\frac{5}{6}$ of $\frac{1}{3}$ of 27

2) $1\frac{3}{7} \times 1\frac{1}{20}$ 7) $\frac{9}{10}$ of $2\frac{2}{3}$ 12) $\frac{7}{12} \times 3\frac{1}{5} \times 1\frac{7}{8}$

3) $\frac{2}{5}$ of $\frac{3}{7}$ 8) $\frac{5}{6} \times 5\frac{1}{4}$ 13) $2\frac{2}{9} \times \frac{3}{11} \times 1\frac{1}{10}$

4) $8 \times \frac{5}{12}$ 9) $4\frac{4}{7} \times 1\frac{1}{6}$ 14) $\frac{3}{16}$ of $\frac{1}{3}$ of $4\frac{4}{5}$

5) $4\frac{4}{5} \times 3\frac{3}{4}$ 10) $\frac{1}{5}$ of $3\frac{1}{3}$ 15) $1\frac{1}{2} \times 1\frac{1}{2} \times 1\frac{1}{2}$

---

d

1) $1\frac{1}{14} \times 2\frac{1}{10}$ 11) Multiply $\frac{3}{8}$ by $1\frac{7}{9}$

2) $7\frac{2}{7} \times 1\frac{4}{17}$ 12) Multiply $1\frac{1}{15}$ by $1\frac{1}{8}$

3) $2\frac{1}{5} \times 1\frac{1}{6}$ 13) Multiply $2\frac{1}{10}$ by $2\frac{2}{7}$

4) $4\frac{1}{2} \times 2\frac{2}{5}$ 14) Multiply $4\frac{1}{5}$ by $1\frac{3}{8}$

5) $6\frac{3}{4} \times 1\frac{1}{9}$ 15) Multiply $\frac{1}{6}$ by $7\frac{1}{2}$

6) $\frac{7}{12} \times 7\frac{1}{5}$ 16) Find the product of $5\frac{3}{5}$ and $1\frac{4}{21}$

7) $3\frac{7}{16} \times 2\frac{6}{11}$ 17) Find the product of $1\frac{4}{5}$ and $\frac{1}{12}$

8) $11\frac{1}{4} \times 3\frac{1}{3}$ 18) Find the product of $\frac{22}{25}$ and $1\frac{7}{8}$

9) $\frac{1}{99} \times 7\frac{7}{10}$ 19) Find the product of 6, $1\frac{2}{3}$ and $\frac{7}{10}$

10) $5\frac{2}{5} \times 7\frac{11}{12}$ 20) Find the product of $\frac{5}{8}$, $\frac{4}{11}$ and $\frac{11}{15}$

 **DIVISION**

DIVISION is just like multiplication except for an important extra rule (*2)

e.g. $3\frac{3}{5} \div 2\frac{1}{10}$

*1) Turn any mixed numbers to IMPROPER (top-heavy) fractions

$\frac{18}{5} \div \frac{21}{10}$

*2) TURN RIGHT-HAND FRACTION UPSIDE-DOWN CHANGE ÷ TO X

$\frac{18}{5}$ X $\frac{10}{21}$

*3) Cancel if you can

$\frac{^{6}\cancel{18}}{_{1}\cancel{5}}$ X $\frac{\cancel{10}^{\,2}}{\cancel{21}\,_{7}}$

*4) Multiply (top x top, bottom x bottom)

$\frac{12}{7}$

*5) If improper (top-heavy) change to mixed number

$1\frac{5}{7}$

B If you are given a problem like

$$\frac{1\frac{1}{2}}{1\frac{5}{6}} \longleftarrow \text{this line means DIVIDE}$$

so set it out as a division and go on as usual

$1\frac{1}{2} \div 1\frac{5}{6}$

$\frac{3}{2} \div \frac{11}{6}$

$\frac{3}{2}$ X $\frac{6}{11}$

$\frac{3}{_{1}\cancel{2}}$ X $\frac{\cancel{6}^{\,3}}{11}$

$\frac{9}{11}$

a

1) $\frac{2}{5} \div \frac{3}{5}$ 6) $\frac{5}{6} \div \frac{2}{3}$ 11) $\frac{7}{10} \div \frac{3}{5}$ 16) $1\frac{1}{2} \div 1\frac{1}{5}$

2) $\frac{1}{8} \div \frac{3}{4}$ 7) $\frac{1}{4} \div \frac{5}{8}$ 12) $1\frac{1}{2} \div \frac{2}{3}$ 17) $1\frac{1}{3} \div 2\frac{1}{2}$

3) $\frac{3}{5} \div \frac{1}{10}$ 8) $\frac{2}{3} \div 1\frac{5}{6}$ 13) $\frac{3}{4} \div 1\frac{1}{8}$ 18) $3\frac{3}{4} \div 1\frac{1}{5}$

4) $\frac{1}{2} \div \frac{7}{8}$ 9) $\frac{7}{8} \div \frac{7}{8}$ 14) $1\frac{5}{6} \div \frac{1}{3}$ 19) $3\frac{1}{4} \div 4\frac{1}{3}$

5) $\frac{3}{8} \div \frac{1}{2}$ 10) $2\frac{1}{3} \div \frac{5}{6}$ 15) $2\frac{2}{3} \div \frac{2}{3}$ 20) $1\frac{1}{4} \div \frac{10}{11}$

b

1) $4\frac{2}{5} \div 3\frac{3}{10}$ 6) $1\frac{3}{4} \div \frac{7}{10}$ 11) $2\frac{2}{3} \div \frac{1}{4}$ 16) $3\frac{3}{4} \div 1\frac{4}{5}$

2) $1\frac{3}{4} \div 4\frac{1}{5}$ 7) $5\frac{2}{3} \div 1\frac{1}{6}$ 12) $1\frac{2}{5} \div 1\frac{3}{11}$ 17) $4\frac{1}{8} \div 2\frac{3}{4}$

3) $5\frac{4}{5} \div \frac{4}{5}$ 8) $3\frac{3}{5} \div 2\frac{1}{10}$ 13) $2\frac{3}{5} \div 5\frac{1}{5}$ 18) $3\frac{1}{7} \div 5\frac{1}{2}$

4) $\frac{1}{32} \div \frac{5}{8}$ 9) $4\frac{2}{3} \div \frac{7}{8}$ 14) $1\frac{5}{6} \div 3\frac{1}{7}$ 19) $4\frac{1}{2} \div 1\frac{1}{2}$

5) $1\frac{1}{3} \div \frac{2}{9}$ 10) $5\frac{1}{4} \div 2\frac{3}{16}$ 15) $3\frac{1}{9} \div 1\frac{1}{6}$ 20) $3\frac{5}{6} \div 1\frac{1}{2}$

c

Write any whole numbers as fractions,
e.g. Write 2 as $\frac{2}{1}$, 5 as $\frac{5}{1}$, 14 as $\frac{14}{1}$, etc.

1) $3\frac{1}{5} \div 1\frac{7}{15}$ 6) $5\frac{1}{4} \div 7$ 11) $1 \div 3\frac{1}{3}$ 16) $2\frac{2}{9} \div 1\frac{2}{3}$

2) $2\frac{5}{8} \div 4\frac{2}{3}$ 7) $3\frac{3}{4} \div 4\frac{2}{7}$ 12) $3\frac{1}{4} \div 4\frac{1}{3}$ 17) $6\frac{2}{3} \div \frac{5}{9}$

3) $3 \div 1\frac{1}{4}$ 8) $3\frac{1}{5} \div 4$ 13) $1\frac{1}{4} \div \frac{5}{6}$ 18) $12 \div 3\frac{3}{4}$

4) $1\frac{1}{2} \div 1\frac{1}{5}$ 9) $12\frac{1}{4} \div 3\frac{1}{2}$ 14) $\frac{1}{12} \div 1\frac{1}{4}$ 19) $4\frac{1}{6} \div 10$

5) $3\frac{1}{3} \div 5$ 10) $15 \div 3$ 15) $4 \div 2\frac{1}{5}$ 20) $1\frac{5}{7} \div 1\frac{7}{8}$

d

1) $\dfrac{\frac{1}{4}}{\frac{3}{4}}$ 4) $\dfrac{\frac{5}{6}}{2\frac{1}{12}}$ 7) $\dfrac{1\frac{3}{10}}{\frac{4}{5}}$ 10) $\dfrac{5\frac{5}{6}}{1\frac{1}{4}}$ 13) $\dfrac{2\frac{1}{4}}{1\frac{3}{8}}$

2) $\dfrac{3\frac{1}{3}}{2\frac{1}{2}}$ 5) $\dfrac{2\frac{5}{8}}{14}$ 8) $\dfrac{\frac{7}{10}}{\frac{2}{5}}$ 11) $\dfrac{10}{1\frac{2}{3}}$ 14) $\dfrac{\frac{7}{8}}{4\frac{2}{3}}$

3) $\dfrac{\frac{5}{16}}{\frac{1}{4}}$ 6) $\dfrac{1\frac{2}{3}}{1\frac{3}{7}}$ 9) $\dfrac{5\frac{1}{4}}{1\frac{1}{2}}$ 12) $\dfrac{3\frac{3}{4}}{2\frac{2}{3}}$ 15) $\dfrac{8}{\frac{1}{4}}$

$\mathbf{A}$ X ÷ MULTIPLICATION AND DIVISION

e.g. $3\frac{1}{4} \times 1\frac{7}{10} \div 5\frac{1}{5}$

*1) Turn any mixed numbers into IMPROPER fractions

$\frac{13}{4}$ X $\frac{17}{10}$ ÷ $\frac{26}{5}$

*2) INVERT (turn upside-down) any **division** and change ÷ to x

$\frac{13}{4}$ X $\frac{17}{10}$ **X** $\frac{5}{26}$

*3) Cancel if you can

$\frac{\cancel{13}^1}{4}$ X $\frac{17}{\cancel{10}_2}$ X $\frac{\cancel{5}^1}{\cancel{26}_2}$

*4) Multiply (top x top, bottom x bottom)

$\frac{17}{16}$

*5) If improper (top-heavy) change to a mixed number

$1\frac{1}{16}$

---

e.g. (2)

$2\frac{2}{3} \div \frac{4}{5} \times 1\frac{1}{8}$

$\frac{8}{3} \div \frac{4}{5} \times \frac{9}{8}$

$\frac{8}{3}$ **X** $\frac{5}{4}$ **X** $\frac{9}{8}$

$\frac{\cancel{8}^1}{\cancel{3}_1} \times \frac{5}{4} \times \frac{\cancel{9}^3}{\cancel{8}_1}$

$\frac{15}{4}$

$3\frac{3}{4}$

e.g. (3)

$3\frac{1}{8} \div 1\frac{1}{4} \div 2\frac{6}{7}$

$\frac{25}{8} \div \frac{5}{4} \div \frac{20}{7}$

$\frac{25}{8}$ **X** $\frac{4}{5}$ **X** $\frac{7}{20}$

$\frac{\cancel{25}^5}{\cancel{8}_2} \times \frac{\cancel{4}^1}{\cancel{5}_1} \times \frac{7}{\cancel{20}_4}$

$\frac{7}{8}$

B If you are given a problem like

$$\frac{1\frac{2}{3} \times \frac{4}{5}}{\frac{1}{3} \times 1\frac{1}{4}}$$ ← this line means DIVIDE

*1) Work out the top

$1\frac{2}{3} \times \frac{4}{5} = \frac{4}{3}$

*2) Work out the bottom

$\frac{1}{3} \times 1\frac{1}{4} = \frac{5}{12}$

*3) DIVIDE top by bottom

$\frac{4}{5} \div \frac{5}{12} = 3\frac{1}{5}$

a

1) $\frac{3}{10} \times 3\frac{1}{3}$ 6) $3\frac{3}{4} \times 1\frac{4}{5}$ 11) $5\frac{1}{3} \div 4$

2) $6\frac{3}{4} \div \frac{9}{10}$ 7) $2\frac{1}{12} \div 2\frac{1}{3}$ 12) $\frac{5}{6} \times 5\frac{1}{5}$

3) $1\frac{1}{9} \times 3\frac{3}{8}$ 8) $10 \div \frac{5}{12}$ 13) $3\frac{3}{5} \times \frac{3}{4}$

4) $4\frac{2}{3} \times 2\frac{1}{7}$ 9) $1\frac{4}{7} \times 2\frac{2}{3}$ 14) $1\frac{2}{7} \times 5\frac{5}{6}$

5) $4\frac{1}{6} \div 1\frac{2}{3}$ 10) $5\frac{1}{9} \div 3\frac{5}{6}$ 15) $\frac{20}{21} \div 1\frac{1}{14}$

b

1) $\frac{2}{3} \times \frac{1}{4} \div \frac{5}{9}$ 6) $1\frac{1}{6} \div \frac{5}{8} \times 2\frac{1}{7}$

2) $1\frac{3}{5} \times \frac{2}{3} \times 1\frac{1}{4}$ 7) $8\frac{3}{4} \div 1\frac{7}{8} \div \frac{5}{6}$

3) $\frac{1}{4} \div \frac{1}{5} \times \frac{1}{3}$ 8) $2\frac{2}{3} \times \frac{1}{2} \div 1\frac{3}{5}$

4) $1\frac{1}{3} \div \frac{7}{15} \div 2$ 9) $6 \div \frac{2}{3} \div 5$

5) $5\frac{1}{2} \times \frac{9}{10} \div 4\frac{2}{5}$ 10) $\frac{9}{10} \times 6\frac{1}{4} \div \frac{3}{7}$

11) Divide by $5\frac{1}{3}$ the product of $\frac{4}{5}$ and $3\frac{1}{3}$

12) Find the product of $2\frac{5}{8}$ and $(3\frac{2}{7} \div 5\frac{3}{4})$

13) Multiply by $1\frac{1}{2}$ the result of dividing $2\frac{2}{3}$ by 4

14) Divide $8\frac{1}{4}$ by the product of $1\frac{5}{6}$ and $\frac{3}{5}$

15) Multiply the product of $\frac{7}{8}$ and $\frac{5}{8}$ by $\frac{3}{8}$

c

1) $\dfrac{1\frac{2}{3} \times \frac{7}{10}}{2\frac{4}{5}}$ 5) $\dfrac{3\frac{9}{10} \div 6\frac{1}{2}}{\frac{7}{15}}$ 9) $\dfrac{8}{\frac{2}{3} \times 3\frac{1}{5}}$

2) $\dfrac{2\frac{1}{2} \div 1\frac{1}{3}}{2\frac{1}{12}}$ 6) $\dfrac{\frac{5}{12} \div \frac{7}{8}}{\frac{5}{8} \times \frac{1}{3}}$ 10) $\dfrac{5\frac{1}{4} \times \frac{2}{3}}{\frac{1}{4} \times 1\frac{1}{2}}$

3) $\dfrac{4\frac{1}{5}}{\frac{2}{3} \times \frac{7}{10}}$ 7) $\dfrac{4\frac{2}{3} \times 3\frac{1}{7}}{2\frac{1}{5}}$

4) $\dfrac{3\frac{2}{5} \times 1\frac{2}{3}}{1\frac{1}{3} \times 4\frac{1}{4}}$ 8) $\dfrac{6\frac{3}{5}}{6\frac{2}{3} \div \frac{10}{11}}$

A ✛ ━ ✘ ÷ MIXED

WITH BRACKETS

e.g.

*1) Always do the parts INSIDE the brackets first

*2) Then do the other parts

$$(2\tfrac{2}{3} + 3\tfrac{1}{6}) \div 5\tfrac{1}{4}$$

$$(\tfrac{8}{3} + \tfrac{19}{6}) \div 5\tfrac{1}{4}$$

$$(\tfrac{16}{6} + \tfrac{19}{6}) \div 5\tfrac{1}{4}$$

$$\tfrac{35}{6} \div 5\tfrac{1}{4}$$

$$\tfrac{35}{6} \div \tfrac{21}{4}$$

$$\tfrac{\cancel{35}^{5}}{\cancel{6}_{3}} \times \tfrac{\cancel{4}^{2}}{\cancel{21}_{3}}$$

$$\tfrac{10}{9}$$

$$1\tfrac{1}{9}$$

B WITHOUT BRACKETS

e.g.

*1) Always do x or ÷ first

*2) Then do + or −

$$1\tfrac{1}{3} - \tfrac{3}{10} \times 2\tfrac{1}{2}$$

$$1\tfrac{1}{3} - \tfrac{3}{10} \times \tfrac{5}{2}$$

$$1\tfrac{1}{3} - \tfrac{3}{\cancel{10}_{2}} \times \tfrac{\cancel{5}^{1}}{2}$$

$$1\tfrac{1}{3} - \tfrac{3}{4}$$

$$1 \quad \tfrac{1}{3} - \tfrac{3}{4}$$

$$\tfrac{12}{12} + \tfrac{4}{12} - \tfrac{9}{12}$$

$$\tfrac{7}{12}$$

C If you are given a problem like

$$\frac{2\tfrac{3}{4} + 1\tfrac{1}{3}}{1\tfrac{1}{3} - \tfrac{2}{5}} \quad \longleftarrow \text{ this line means DIVIDE}$$

*1) Work out the top

*2) Work out the bottom

*3) DIVIDE top by bottom

$$2\tfrac{3}{4} + 1\tfrac{1}{3} = 4\tfrac{1}{12}$$

$$1\tfrac{1}{3} - \tfrac{2}{5} = \tfrac{14}{15}$$

$$4\tfrac{1}{12} \div \tfrac{14}{15} = 4\tfrac{3}{8}$$

D REMEMBER 'B O M D A S'

First   **B**rackets

Then   **O**f, **M**ultiply, **D**ivide

Then   **A**dd, **S**ubtract

a

1) $2\frac{1}{4} + 3\frac{2}{3}$ 6) $2\frac{3}{4} \div 3\frac{1}{7}$ 11) $3\frac{3}{10} - 1\frac{2}{5}$ 16) $2\frac{1}{12} \div 3\frac{3}{4}$

2) $1\frac{7}{8} \times 3\frac{3}{5}$ 7) $1\frac{7}{8} + 4\frac{1}{4}$ 12) $\frac{5}{8} \times 4\frac{2}{3}$ 17) $1\frac{1}{8} - \frac{3}{5}$

3) $1\frac{2}{3} \div 2\frac{2}{9}$ 8) $4\frac{1}{3} - \frac{5}{6}$ 13) $3\frac{1}{5} \div \frac{14}{15}$ 18) $3\frac{1}{5} \times 1\frac{1}{4}$

4) $2\frac{5}{6} - \frac{1}{4}$ 9) $2\frac{3}{4} \times 3$ 14) $6 - 2\frac{2}{9}$ 19) $2\frac{1}{2} + \frac{5}{8}$

5) $1\frac{5}{7} \times 2\frac{5}{8}$ 10) $3\frac{2}{5} + 1\frac{1}{4}$ 15) $2\frac{1}{3} + 1\frac{3}{5}$ 20) $4\frac{1}{2} \div 1\frac{7}{8}$

b

1) $(\frac{1}{4} + \frac{1}{3}) \times \frac{4}{5}$ 6) $1\frac{1}{20} \div (1\frac{1}{2} + 1\frac{1}{5})$

2) $3\frac{2}{5} \div (2\frac{1}{2} + \frac{1}{3})$ 7) $(4\frac{1}{2} - 1\frac{3}{4}) \div 7\frac{1}{3}$

3) $(1\frac{1}{2} + 2\frac{2}{3}) \times 1\frac{1}{15}$ 8) $3\frac{1}{7} \div 1\frac{3}{8} + \frac{1}{2}$

4) $1\frac{1}{10} \times (\frac{3}{4} - \frac{1}{3})$ 9) $4\frac{1}{6} \times (\frac{7}{8} - \frac{4}{5})$

5) $3\frac{1}{3} - (\frac{5}{6} + 2\frac{1}{2})$ 10) $(\frac{3}{5} + 1\frac{1}{2}) \times 3$

c

1) $(1\frac{1}{6} - \frac{5}{9}) \div 1\frac{2}{3}$

2) $6\frac{2}{3} \times (1\frac{5}{8} - \frac{4}{5})$

3) $(4\frac{5}{6} + 2\frac{1}{2}) \times 4\frac{1}{2}$

4) $3\frac{7}{8} \div (4\frac{4}{9} + 1\frac{7}{12})$

5) $(3\frac{5}{6} + 1\frac{1}{2}) \times (1\frac{1}{6} - \frac{3}{4})$

6) $\dfrac{1\frac{1}{2} + 2\frac{1}{10}}{3\frac{3}{5}}$

7) $\dfrac{\frac{2}{3} - \frac{1}{5}}{\frac{11}{20} + 2\frac{1}{4}}$

8) $\dfrac{\frac{1}{7} + \frac{1}{4}}{3\frac{3}{10}}$

9) $\dfrac{2\frac{4}{5} \div 3\frac{1}{2}}{\frac{1}{3} \times 1\frac{2}{5}}$

10) $\dfrac{2\frac{5}{8}}{2\frac{1}{2} - 1\frac{1}{3}}$

d

1) Multiply by $1\frac{7}{8}$ the sum of $1\frac{1}{5}$ and $2\frac{2}{3}$

2) Add $1\frac{3}{4}$ to the product of $2\frac{1}{4}$ and $1\frac{5}{6}$

3) Subtract $\frac{3}{4}$ from the sum of $\frac{7}{10}$ and $1\frac{3}{5}$

4) Multiply by $1\frac{4}{5}$ the difference between $2\frac{1}{4}$ and $\frac{7}{12}$

5) From the product of $5\frac{1}{3}$ and $\frac{5}{8}$ subtract $3\frac{1}{3}$

6) Divide by $5\frac{1}{5}$ the sum of $1\frac{1}{5}$ and $\frac{3}{4}$

7) Add $\frac{1}{2}$ to the product of $\frac{4}{9}$ and $3\frac{3}{5}$

8) Multiply the sum of $4\frac{1}{2}$ and $5\frac{3}{10}$ by $1\frac{3}{7}$

9) Divide the difference between $3\frac{2}{5}$ and $\frac{2}{3}$ by $5\frac{1}{8}$

10) Subtract $\frac{5}{6}$ from the product of $1\frac{7}{8}$ and $\frac{4}{5}$

A CHANGING FRACTIONS TO DECIMALS

*1) Make the top (numerator) look like a decimal by writing .0 after it

e.g. $\frac{3}{4}$

$\frac{3.0}{4}$

*2) Divide the top (numerator) by the bottom (denominator) Add extra noughts if necessary

$$\begin{array}{r} .7\,5 \\ 4\,)\overline{3.0^2 0} \end{array}$$

$\frac{3}{4} = 0.75$

Some more examples

$\frac{1}{8}$

$\frac{1.0}{8}$

$$\begin{array}{r} .125 \\ 8\,)\overline{1.000} \end{array}$$

$\frac{1}{8} = 0.125$

$\frac{2}{5}$

$\frac{2.0}{5}$

$$\begin{array}{r} .4 \\ 5\,)\overline{2.0} \end{array}$$

$\frac{2}{5} = 0.4$

$\frac{11}{16}$

$\frac{11.0}{16}$

$$\begin{array}{r} .6875 \\ 16\,)\overline{11.0000} \end{array}$$

$\frac{11}{16} = 0.6875$

B Whole numbers STAY THE SAME
Be careful not to forget the whole numbers

e.g. $2\frac{4}{5}$

$2\frac{4.0}{5}$

$$2 \quad \begin{array}{r} .8 \\ 5\,)\overline{4.0} \end{array}$$

$2\frac{4}{5} = 2.8$

C Some fractions become RECURRING DECIMALS

e.g.

$\frac{8}{9}$

$\frac{8.0}{9}$

$$\begin{array}{r} .888 \text{ etc} \\ 9\,)\overline{8.000} \end{array}$$

$\frac{8}{9} = 0.\dot{8}$

e.g.

$\frac{6}{11}$

$\frac{6.0}{11}$

$$\begin{array}{r} .5454 \text{ etc} \\ 11\,)\overline{6.0000} \end{array}$$

$\frac{6}{11} = 0.\dot{5}\dot{4}$

a

Change these fractions into decimals

1)	$\frac{1}{4}$	6)	$\frac{9}{20}$	11)	$\frac{5}{16}$	16)	$\frac{4}{5}$
2)	$\frac{2}{5}$	7)	$\frac{1}{2}$	12)	$\frac{7}{10}$	17)	$\frac{33}{40}$
3)	$\frac{3}{8}$	8)	$\frac{3}{10}$	13)	$\frac{5}{8}$	18)	$\frac{7}{25}$
4)	$\frac{9}{10}$	9)	$\frac{7}{16}$	14)	$\frac{1}{5}$	19)	$\frac{1}{10}$
5)	$\frac{3}{5}$	10)	$\frac{9}{25}$	15)	$\frac{17}{20}$	20)	$\frac{7}{8}$

b

Change these fractions into decimals. Remember that
WHOLE NUMBERS STAY THE SAME

1)	$2\frac{1}{8}$	6)	$6\frac{3}{4}$	11)	$3\frac{7}{8}$	16)	$\frac{9}{40}$
2)	$4\frac{9}{10}$	7)	$\frac{39}{50}$	12)	$1\frac{7}{10}$	17)	$2\frac{2}{5}$
3)	$3\frac{4}{5}$	8)	$1\frac{5}{8}$	13)	$5\frac{1}{4}$	18)	$\frac{3}{20}$
4)	$\frac{11}{25}$	9)	$4\frac{1}{5}$	14)	$8\frac{7}{10}$	19)	$2\frac{1}{16}$
5)	$12\frac{1}{2}$	10)	$\frac{9}{16}$	15)	$\frac{3}{25}$	20)	$7\frac{3}{5}$

c

Change these fractions into recurring decimals

1)	$\frac{1}{9}$	6)	$2\frac{2}{9}$	11)	$\frac{7}{15}$	16)	$1\frac{8}{11}$
2)	$\frac{2}{3}$	7)	$\frac{5}{12}$	12)	$\frac{10}{11}$	17)	$\frac{4}{15}$
3)	$\frac{5}{6}$	8)	$2\frac{1}{11}$	13)	$5\frac{1}{6}$	18)	$4\frac{3}{7}$
4)	$\frac{4}{11}$	9)	$1\frac{1}{3}$	14)	$\frac{5}{18}$	19)	$5\frac{2}{3}$
5)	$\frac{7}{12}$	10)	$\frac{11}{30}$	15)	$\frac{1}{7}$	20)	$\frac{4}{13}$

d

Change these fractions into decimals. Some will be
recurring.

1)	$1\frac{3}{10}$	6)	$\frac{15}{16}$	11)	$5\frac{9}{10}$	16)	$\frac{69}{100}$
2)	$2\frac{1}{4}$	7)	$9\frac{3}{4}$	12)	$23\frac{1}{2}$	17)	$\frac{19}{20}$
3)	$3\frac{2}{3}$	8)	$4\frac{5}{6}$	13)	$\frac{6}{7}$	18)	$1\frac{8}{9}$
4)	$\frac{5}{9}$	9)	$\frac{21}{25}$	14)	$1\frac{3}{8}$	19)	$\frac{11}{12}$
5)	$2\frac{4}{5}$	10)	$6\frac{1}{5}$	15)	$\frac{2}{15}$	20)	$8\frac{1}{8}$

A CHANGING DECIMALS TO FRACTIONS

e.g.   0.65

*1) Make into a WHOLE NUMBER by multiplying (in this case × 100)

65

*2) Put this over the number you have multiplied by

$\dfrac{65}{100}$

*3) Cancel as far as you can

$\dfrac{\cancel{65}^{13}}{\cancel{100}_{20}} = \dfrac{13}{20}$

Some more examples

0.8	0.46	0.125
$\dfrac{8}{10}$	$\dfrac{46}{100}$	$\dfrac{125}{1000}$
$\dfrac{\cancel{8}^{4}}{\cancel{10}_{5}}$	$\dfrac{\cancel{46}^{23}}{\cancel{100}_{50}}$	$\dfrac{\cancel{125}^{1}}{\cancel{1000}_{8}}$
$\dfrac{4}{5}$	$\dfrac{23}{50}$	$\dfrac{1}{8}$

B REMEMBER

If decimal has ONE decimal place (e.g. 0.$\underline{7}$) put over 1$\underline{0}$ ($\frac{7}{10}$)

If decimal has TWO decimal places (e.g. 0.$\underline{2}$ $\underline{1}$) put over 1$\underline{00}$ ($\frac{21}{100}$)

If decimal has THREE decimal places (e.g. 0.$\underline{4}$ $\underline{3}$ $\underline{3}$)
    put over 1 $\underline{0}$ $\underline{0}$ $\underline{0}$ ($\frac{433}{1000}$)

C Whole numbers STAY THE SAME   e.g.   3.4
Be careful not to forget the whole numbers

$3\,\dfrac{\cancel{4}^{2}}{\cancel{10}_{5}}$

$3\,\dfrac{2}{5}$

a Change these decimals into fractions

1) 0.2	*6)* 0.375	*11)* 0.38	*16)* 0.775
2) 0.56	*7)* 0.88	*12)* 0.001	*17)* 0.48
3) 0.7	*8)* 0.975	*13)* 0.9	*18)* 0.15
4) 0.105	*9)* 0.04	*14)* 0.24	*19)* 0.6
5) 0.35	*10)* 0.13	*15)* 0.75	*20)* 0.78

b Express as fractions

1) 0.25	*6)* 0.08	*11)* 0.22	*16)* 0.85
2) 0.112	*7)* 0.625	*12)* 0.002	*17)* 0.1
3) 0.44	*8)* 0.3	*13)* 0.05	*18)* 0.675
4) 0.4	*9)* 0.58	*14)* 0.432	*19)* 0.0006
5) 0.075	*10)* 0.01	*15)* 0.5	*20)* 0.45

c Change these decimals into fractions.
Remember that WHOLE NUMBERS STAY THE SAME

1) 0.96	*6)* 1.95	*11)* 0.875	*16)* 0.416
2) 3.75	*7)* 2.64	*12)* 1.52	*17)* 2.36
3) 1.4	*8)* 3.8	*13)* 0.0625	*18)* 3.275
4) 0.82	*9)* 0.55	*14)* 4.5	*19)* 1.02
5) 4.125	*10)* 6.16	*15)* 0.12	*20)* 8.7

d Express as fractions

1) 5.06	*6)* 0.315	*11)* 0.504	*16)* 4.725
2) 1.92	*7)* 1.32	*12)* 4.28	*17)* 0.008
3) 0.425	*8)* 0.8875	*13)* 3.68	*18)* 0.84
4) 7.9	*9)* 3.2	*14)* 5.475	*19)* 0.7575
5) 0.95	*10)* 8.72	*15)* 14.6	*20)* 12.25

A ARRANGING DECIMALS IN ORDER
OF SIZE   e.g.   Arrange 2.645, 2.189, 3.7 in order
of size, starting with the largest.

*1) Set out in columns

    2 . 6 4 5
    2 . 1 8 9
    3 . 7

*2) Look at largest column

    2 . 6 4 5
    2 . 1 8 9
    3 . 7

3 is the largest in this column, so 3.7 is the largest

The others are both 2, so

*3) Look at the next column

    2 . 6 4 5
    2 . 1 8 9

6 is larger than 1, so 2.645 is next. The order is 3.7, 2.645, 2.189.

B ARRANGING FRACTIONS IN ORDER
OF SIZE

e.g.   Arrange $\frac{1}{4}$, $\frac{5}{16}$, $\frac{6}{25}$, $\frac{3}{11}$ in order of size
starting with the largest.

*1) Change to DECIMALS
(see page 50) and
set out in columns

$\frac{1}{4}$ = 0.25

$\frac{5}{16}$ = 0.3125

$\frac{6}{25}$ = 0.24

$\frac{3}{11}$ = 0.27272

*2) In largest column, every figure is 0, so
look at next column

    0 . 2 5
    0 . 3 1 2 5
    0 . 2 4
    0 . 2 7 2 7 2

3 is larger than 2, so 0.3125 is largest. The others are all 2, so

*3) Look at next column.
7 is largest of these
5 is next
4 is next

    0 . 2 5
    0 . 2 4
    0 . 2 7 2 7 2

The order is 0.3125, 0.27272, 0.25, 0.24

or $\frac{5}{16}$, $\frac{3}{11}$, $\frac{1}{4}$, $\frac{6}{25}$

a

Arrange the numbers in each of these groups in order of size, starting with the LARGEST

1) 5.3, 4.2, 6.0, 3.1

2) 2.4, 1.8, 2.6, 2.3

3) 0.76, 1.3, 0.81

4) 19.2, 18.56, 20.8, 19.7

5) 4.35, 4.32, 4.29, 4.19

6) 20.79, 35.6, 31.23, 48.7

7) 13.25, 21.08, 13.27, 12.92

8) 0.72, 0.78, 0.27

9) 2.58, 2.78, 2.5, 2.87

10) 8.02, 7.36, 7.19, 7.33

11) 0.45, 0.4, 0.54, 0.48, 0.5

12) 8.8, 8.08, 0.88, 8.808

13) 6.37, 6.39, 6.375, 6.4

14) 0.193, 0.182, 0.181, 0.191, 0.187

15) 0.5454, 0.532, 0.545, 0.5326

b

Arrange the fractions in each of these groups in order of size starting with the LARGEST

1) $\frac{3}{4}$, $\frac{4}{5}$, $\frac{1}{10}$

2) $\frac{2}{3}$, $\frac{7}{10}$, $\frac{1}{2}$

3) $\frac{1}{5}$, $\frac{1}{8}$, $\frac{3}{10}$

4) $\frac{3}{20}$, $\frac{2}{9}$, $\frac{1}{5}$

5) $\frac{7}{9}$, $\frac{5}{6}$, $\frac{9}{10}$

6) $\frac{6}{11}$, $\frac{5}{8}$, $\frac{3}{5}$, $\frac{1}{2}$

7) $\frac{3}{7}$, $\frac{2}{5}$, $\frac{1}{2}$, $\frac{9}{20}$

8) $\frac{9}{10}$, $\frac{21}{25}$, $\frac{17}{20}$

9) $\frac{9}{16}$, $\frac{11}{20}$, $\frac{13}{25}$

10) $\frac{17}{50}$, $\frac{3}{8}$, $\frac{1}{3}$, $\frac{7}{20}$

11) $\frac{3}{20}$, $\frac{2}{11}$, $\frac{1}{8}$

12) $\frac{8}{9}$, $\frac{22}{25}$, $\frac{7}{8}$

13) $\frac{5}{9}$, $\frac{3}{5}$, $\frac{12}{25}$, $\frac{4}{7}$

14) $\frac{7}{10}$, $\frac{7}{9}$, $\frac{3}{4}$, $\frac{18}{25}$

15) $1\frac{1}{2}$, $2\frac{1}{4}$, $\frac{3}{8}$, $1\frac{3}{5}$

16) $\frac{4}{5}$, $\frac{17}{20}$, $\frac{6}{7}$

17) $\frac{23}{25}$, $\frac{9}{10}$, $\frac{15}{16}$

18) $\frac{1}{2}$, $\frac{4}{7}$, $\frac{8}{15}$, $\frac{7}{12}$

19) $\frac{5}{18}$, $\frac{3}{11}$, $\frac{11}{40}$

20) $\frac{5}{12}$, $\frac{4}{9}$, $\frac{3}{8}$, $\frac{9}{20}$

c

Arrange the numbers in each of these groups in order of size starting with the SMALLEST

1) $\frac{3}{5}$, $\frac{2}{3}$, $\frac{7}{11}$, $\frac{13}{20}$

2) $\frac{11}{16}$, $\frac{17}{25}$, $\frac{7}{10}$

3) 1.32, 1.23, 1.3, 1.26

4) $\frac{17}{20}$, $\frac{6}{7}$, $\frac{11}{13}$

5) $\frac{1}{6}$, $\frac{4}{25}$, 0.155, $\frac{3}{20}$

6) 921, 1219, 219, 2191

7) $4\frac{5}{9}$, 4.59, $4\frac{3}{5}$, 4.53

8) $\frac{4}{11}$, $\frac{3}{8}$, 0.31, $\frac{1}{3}$

9) 11000, 1010, 10101, 1100

10) $\frac{10}{13}$, $\frac{3}{4}$, $\frac{5}{7}$

11) 0.032, 0.0302, 0.0032, 0.3

12) $\frac{8}{9}$, $\frac{9}{11}$, $\frac{13}{16}$

13) 0.085, $\frac{1}{12}$, 0.084

14) 53.6999, 53.694, 53.6995, 53.7

15) $\frac{3}{8}$, $\frac{7}{18}$, $\frac{4}{11}$, $\frac{9}{25}$, $\frac{5}{13}$

A CHANGING FRACTIONS TO PERCENTAGES (%)

e.g. $\frac{3}{4}$

* Multiply by 100

Do not forget to write the % sign

$\frac{3}{4}$ x $\frac{100}{1}$

$\frac{3}{4}$ x $\frac{100^{25}}{1}$

75%

Other examples

$\frac{1}{8}$

$\frac{1}{8}$ x $\frac{100^{25}}{1}$

$\frac{25}{2}$

$12\frac{1}{2}$ %

$1\frac{4}{5}$

$\frac{9}{5}$ x $\frac{100^{20}}{1}$

$\frac{180}{1}$

180%

$\frac{4}{9}$

$\frac{4}{9}$ x $\frac{100}{1}$

$\frac{400}{9}$

$44\frac{4}{9}$ %

B CHANGING DECIMALS TO PERCENTAGES (%)

e.g. 0.54

* Multiply by 100
Do not forget to write the % sign

0.54 x 100

54%

Other examples

0.7	0.925	1.43
0.7 x 100	0.925 x 100	1.43 x 100
70%	92.5%	143%

C EXPRESSING A NUMBER AS A PERCENTAGE OF ANOTHER NUMBER

e.g. Express 4 as a percentage of 15

*1) Write the first number OVER the second number as a fraction

$\frac{4}{15}$

*2) Multiply by 100

$\frac{4}{15}$ x $\frac{100^{20}}{1}$

$\frac{80}{3}$

$26\frac{2}{3}$ %

a Write these fractions as percentages

1) $\frac{2}{5}$ 6) $\frac{21}{25}$ 11) $\frac{1}{2}$ 16) $3\frac{7}{10}$

2) $\frac{37}{100}$ 7) $\frac{3}{8}$ 12) $\frac{14}{15}$ 17) $\frac{9}{25}$

3) $\frac{1}{4}$ 8) $\frac{13}{20}$ 13) $1\frac{1}{20}$ 18) $\frac{27}{40}$

4) $\frac{7}{20}$ 9) $\frac{5}{12}$ 14) $\frac{5}{8}$ 19) $1\frac{1}{10}$

5) $\frac{1}{3}$ 10) $\frac{9}{10}$ 15) $2\frac{3}{5}$ 20) $\frac{99}{100}$

---

b Write these decimals as percentages

1) 0.6   6) 0.98   11) 1.3   16) 0.274

2) 0.25   7) 0.2   12) 0.785   17) 1.59

3) 0.875   8) 0.1325   13) 0.86   18) 0.001

4) 0.39   9) 0.44   14) 0.52   19) 1.04

5) 0.02   10) 0.13   15) 2.15   20) 0.9

---

c
1) Express 3 as a percentage of 10
2) Express 41 as a percentage of 50
3) Express 17 as a percentage of 20
4) Express 8 as a percentage of 16
5) Express 1 as a percentage of 25
6) Express 35 as a percentage of 56
7) Express 15 as a percentage of 75
8) Express 10 ½ as a percentage of 14
9) Express 464 as a percentage of 400
10) Express 162 as a percentage of 720

---

d
1) John scored 16 marks out of 20. What percentage was this?
2) Write £9 as a percentage of £15.
3) Out of 240 marbles, 156 were red. What percentage were red?
4) Express 3.5 as a percentage of 70
5) There were 720 children in a crowd of 1600. What percentage of the crowd were children?
6) What is 84 as a percentage of 90?
7) Of 175 passengers in an airliner, 56 were Americans. What percentage were Americans?
8) In a certain book, 18 of the 25 pictures are in colour. What percentage are in colour?
9) Out of 25 trains arriving at a station, 8 were late. What percentage of the trains were NOT late?
10) Of a class of 20 pupils, 17 were present. What percentage were absent?

A CHANGING PERCENTAGES TO FRACTIONS

e.g. 68%

*1) Write the percentage OVER 100

$$\frac{68}{100}$$

*2) Cancel as far as you can

$$\frac{\cancel{68}^{\,17}}{\cancel{100}_{\,25}}$$

$$\frac{17}{25}$$

B CHANGING FRACTION PERCENTAGES TO FRACTIONS

e.g. $27\frac{1}{2}\%$

*1) Write the percentage OVER 100

$$\frac{27\frac{1}{2}}{100}$$

*2) Multiply top and bottom by the denominator of the fraction.

$$\frac{27\frac{1}{2} \times 2}{100 \times 2} = \frac{55}{200}$$

*3) Cancel as far as you can

$$\frac{\cancel{55}^{\,11}}{\cancel{200}_{\,40}}$$

$$\frac{11}{\mathbf{40}}$$

e.g. (2) 11¼ %

$$\frac{11\frac{1}{4}}{100}$$

$$\frac{11\frac{1}{4} \times 4}{100 \times 4} = \frac{45}{400}$$

$$\frac{\cancel{45}}{\cancel{400}} = \frac{9}{80}$$

e.g. (3) 16⅔ %

$$\frac{16\frac{2}{3}}{100}$$

$$\frac{16\frac{2}{3} \times 3}{100 \times 3} = \frac{50}{300}$$

$$\frac{\cancel{50}}{\cancel{300}} = \frac{1}{6}$$

C CHANGING PERCENTAGES TO DECIMALS

e.g. 72%

*Divide by 100 (see page 14)

$$72 \div 100$$
$$0 \cdot 72$$

If the percentage contains a fraction, change it all to a decimal, and then divide by 100

a Change these percentages to fractions

1) 20%	6) 29%	11) 24%	16) 76%
2) 75%	7) 60%	12) 2%	17) 99%
3) 34%	8) 85%	13) 44%	18) 7½%
4) 90%	9) 4%	14) 10%	19) 50%
5) 15%	10) 81%	15) 35%	20) 65%

---

b Express as fractions

1) 25%	6) 31¼%	11) 73⅓%	16) 50⅖%
2) 1%	7) 28%	12) 5%	17) 12%
3) 45%	8) 62½%	13) 77%	18) 70%
4) 80%	9) 33⅓%	14) 47½%	19) 87½%
5) 22½%	10) 9%	15) 100%	20) 68¾%

---

c Write these percentages as fractions. If your answer is an IMPROPER (top-heavy) fraction, change it to a mixed number — see page 26

1) 72%	6) 91⅔%	11) 83⅓%	16) 48%
2) 140%	7) 275%	12) ½%	17) 12½%
3) 53⅓%	8) 30%	13) 284%	18) 58¾%
4) 82½%	9) 155%	14) 76⅔%	19) 320%
5) 95%	10) 37½%	(15) 17½%	20) 58⅓%

---

d Write these percentages as decimals

1) 62%	6) 105%	11) 6.5%	16) 38.9%
2) 79%	7) 88%	12) 140%	17) 18¼%
3) 18%	8) 43.7%	13) 17½%	18) 222%
4) 54%	9) 98%	14) 59.75%	19) 50%
5) 3%	10) 13%	15) 1%	20) 27%

A FINDING x% OF A NUMBER

e.g.   32% of 67

*1) Write again, with the percentage as a fraction over 100 Remember OF means x

$$\frac{32}{100} \times \frac{67}{1}$$

*2) Work out. It is usually better to LEAVE 100 at the bottom rather than cancelling

$$\frac{32 \times 67}{100 \times 1} = \frac{2144}{100}$$

*3) Divide top by bottom

$$2144 \div 100$$
$$21.44$$

---

e.g. (2)   6% of 91

$$\frac{6}{100} \times \frac{91}{1}$$

$$\frac{546}{100}$$

$$5.46$$

e.g. (3)   75% of £365

$$\frac{75}{100} \times \frac{365}{1}$$

$$\frac{27375}{100}$$

£273.75

B FINDING x% OF NUMBERS WITH FRACTIONS

* These can be done just like the ones at the top of the page, but it sometimes helps to multiply top and bottom first by the same number

e.g. (1) $17\frac{1}{2}$% of £54

$$\frac{17\frac{1}{2}}{100} \times \frac{54}{1}$$

Multiply top and bottom by 2 } $\frac{35}{200} \times \frac{54}{1}$

Then cancel by 2 if possible } $\frac{35}{{}_{100}\cancel{200}} \times \frac{\cancel{54}^{27}}{1}$

$$\frac{945}{100}$$

£9.45

e.g. (2)   56% of $7\frac{1}{4}$

$$\frac{56}{100} \times \frac{7\frac{1}{4}}{1}$$

Multiply top and bottom by 4 } $\frac{56}{100} \times \frac{29}{4}$

Then cancel by 4 if possible } $\frac{\cancel{56}^{14}}{100} \times \frac{29}{\cancel{4}_{1}}$

$$\frac{406}{100}$$

4.06

a

1) 4% of 250	6) 10% of 85	11) 58% of 58
2) 7% of 72	7) 37% of 600	12) 30% of 2
3) 22% of 675	8) 110% of 6	13) 72% of 62.5
4) 15% of 200	9) 9% of 1230	14) 1% of 93
5) 90% of 36	10) 2.5% of 84	15) 88% of 320

b

1) 42% of 150	6) 325% of 20	11) 10 ½ % of 4350
2) 12 ½ % of 64	7) 5 ⅓ % of 714	12) 65% of 118
3) 3% of 2500	8) 17% of 43	13) 2 ¼ % of 960
4) 8 ½ % of 196	9) 5% of 666	14) 38% of 7
5) 120% of 24	10) 42% of 87 ½	15) 6⅔ % of 45

c

Try these. Remember to put the correct units in your answer, e.g. if question is in £, so is answer (35% of £80 = £28); if question is in metres, so is answer (9% of 175 metres = 15.75 metres)

1) 25% of £144	9) 10% of 39.46 litres
2) 7% of 360m	10) 77% of 215 mm
3) 80% of 45p	11) 16 ¼ % of 384 kg
4) 55% of 60 km	12) 11.5% of £6
5) 18% of 28 grams	13) 48% of 130 tonnes
6) 92% of 500 metres	14) 66⅔ % of 12 ha
7) 35% of £95	15) 1 ½ % of £2000
8) 4 ½ % of 300 ml	

d

1) 6% of 51 cm	9) 45% of 60 miles
2) 250% of £8	10) 0.5% of 0.5 mg
3) 18.5% of 420	11) 29% of 67
4) 61% of 43g	12) 90% of 4 ml
5) 33 ⅓ % of 5685 tonnes	13) 12 ½ % of £8500
6) 21% of 7⅔	14) 53% of 14.5
7) 104% of 450 litres	15) 9 ¼ % of £156
8) 82% of $ 775	

A TO INCREASE OR DECREASE BY PERCENTAGE

e.g. INCREASE (make larger)   35 by 40%

Increase is 40% of 35 $= \frac{40}{100} \times \frac{35}{1} = 14$

so answer is 35 + 14 = 49

e.g. DECREASE (make smaller) £125 by 6%

Decrease is 6% of 125 $= \frac{6}{100} \times \frac{125}{1} = 7.5$

so answer is 125 − 7.5 = £117.50

B PERCENTAGE PROFIT AND LOSS

Profit (or **gain** or **increase**)

Percentage profit = $\dfrac{\text{Profit}}{\text{Original amount}} \times \dfrac{100}{1}$

e.g. Mrs. Jones bought an antique vase for £120. Later she sold it for £150. What was her percentage profit?

The profit (extra amount she gained) was

150 − 120 = £30

So **percentage profit** was $\frac{30}{120} \times \frac{100}{1} = 25\%$

Loss (or **decrease**)

Percentage loss $= \dfrac{\text{Loss}}{\text{Original amount}} \times \dfrac{100}{1}$

e.g. Tom bought a car for £4000 and later sold it for £3300. What was his percentage loss?

The loss (amount that Tom lost) was

4000 − 3300 = £700

so **percentage loss** was $\frac{700}{4000} \times \frac{100}{1} = 17\frac{1}{2}\%$

a

1) Increase 48 by 25%
2) Increase 130 by 10%
3) Decrease 500 by 35%
4) Increase 60 by 5%
5) Decrease 250 by 18%
6) Decrease 24 by 12½%
7) Increase 365 by 140%
8) Decrease 72 by 75%

9) Increase £185 by 20%
10) Decrease 64 by 3%
11) Increase 752 by 22½%
12) Decrease £245 by 26%
13) Decrease 9 by 60%
14) Increase 360 by 15%
15) Increase £21 by 33⅓%

---

b

1) John bought a new bicycle for £120. Later he sold it for £90. What was the percentage loss?

2) Mrs Morgan's shop sold cans of cola at 21p each. The cans of cola cost Mrs Morgan 12p each. What percentage profit did she make?

3) A girl put £250 in a bank account. After a year she received £275. What was her percentage gain?

4) What is the percentage profit if a motorbike is bought for £625 and sold for £725?

5) A man bought a horse for £500 and later sold it for £2250. What percentage profit did he make?

6) Nick added 2 new cars to his collection of 40 models. What was the percentage increase in his collection?

7) A cottage was bought for £36000 and sold for £43200. What was the percentage profit?

8) Fiona bought a bracelet for £12.50 and sold it for £10.25. What was her percentage loss?

9) Derek's Transport bought a truck for £8000 and later sold it for £7400. What was the percentage loss?

10) Last year a club had 96 members. This year it has 108. What was the percentage increase in membership?

you bught a Car with 100 and Sold at 80. How much % Profit?

SOME EXTRA QUESTIONS

1) 1428.57×0.7

2) Write 1.45 as a fraction in its lowest terms

3) Divide by 0.9 the sum of 3.3 and 0.84

4) $2\frac{5}{8} \times \frac{5}{7} \div 1\frac{1}{2}$

5) Arrange in order of size, starting with largest
   9.809, 9.908, 9.089, 9.9, 9.890

6) $1\frac{5}{9} \div (1\frac{1}{6} + 1\frac{3}{4})$

7) A man bought a stamp collection for £350 and sold it later for £420. What was the percentage profit?

8) Express $4\frac{3}{16}$ as a decimal

9) What is the sum of 13.13, 9.59 and 7.28?

10) Jane bought a cake. Sally ate $\frac{1}{4}$ of it and Jane ate $\frac{1}{3}$ of it. What fraction of the cake had they eaten?

---

11) $4\frac{1}{5} \times 4\frac{1}{6} + 4\frac{5}{6}$

12) Andrew bought a pair of training shoes at £13.95 a pair, a plastic football at £2.95 and a magazine at 65p. How much did he spend altogether?

13) Express $\frac{37}{40}$ as a percentage

14) Write as a fraction 7.32

15) From the product of 6.5 and 3.8 subtract 9.55

16) Divide by $8\frac{1}{4}$ the difference between $8\frac{1}{2}$ and $1\frac{5}{8}$

17) Find 61% of £625

18) $0.775 + 0.099 - 0.208$

19) Jeremy drank $\frac{4}{5}$ of $\frac{3}{4}$ of $\frac{5}{6}$ of the coffee in his flask. What fraction of the coffee was still left?

20) Divide 0.455 by 1.3 and express your answer as a fraction in its lowest terms

---

21) Express 56% as a fraction in its lowest terms

22) $2\frac{1}{6} + 1\frac{3}{4} - 3\frac{2}{3}$

23) Find the product of 0.026 and 935

24) Kate planned to spend the evening sticking her holiday photographs in an album. She had 45 photographs altogether but by supper time she had stuck in only 36. What fraction of the photographs had she stuck in?

25) Which is the smallest of $\frac{1}{6}$, $\frac{2}{15}$ and $\frac{3}{20}$?

26) $(1.79 + 1.168) \div 3.4$

27) For helping the farmer, Giles and Paul were given £18 to share between them. As Giles had worked harder than Paul, they both agreed that Giles should have $\frac{7}{12}$ of the money and Paul should have the rest of it. How much money did Paul have?

28) Write $3\frac{7}{11}$ as a recurring decimal

29) How much water would there be in 19 containers if each container held 4.55 litres of water?

30) Find $37\frac{1}{2}$% of 56 kilograms

---

31) $11 - 3.7 - 1.92$

32) Find the product of $\frac{3}{8}$ and $7\frac{1}{3}$ and express the answer as a decimal

33) Increase 450 by 14%

34) Find the total cost of 4 tins of beans at 26p each, 3 jars of jam at 37p each and a packet of cornflakes at 39p

35) What is $\frac{2}{3}$ of $\frac{7}{8}$ of 552?

36) Gary is $10\frac{1}{2}$ years old and his Uncle Bob is 28. Express Gary's age as a fraction of Uncle Bob's age.

37) Karen bought a camera in the summer holidays for £25. At the end of the winter term she sold it to a friend for £19. What was the percentage loss?

38) $\dfrac{5\frac{5}{8}}{4\frac{1}{6}}$

39) Multiply the sum of 8.53 and 3.97 by 0.72

40) $(4\frac{1}{2} - 2\frac{4}{7}) \times (1\frac{1}{2} + 2\frac{7}{9})$

---

41) A team played 20 matches and won 14 of them. The other matches were all lost. What percentage of their matches did they LOSE?

42) $\frac{5}{8} \times (5\frac{1}{3} - 1\frac{3}{5})$

43) Express 98 as a percentage of 112

44) Multiply by 0.15 the difference between 0.9 and 0.077

45) $\dfrac{3\frac{2}{3} + 1\frac{5}{6}}{5\frac{4}{5} - 2\frac{1}{2}}$

46) A firm pays all its 16 workers the same wage. Each week the firm pays £1916 wages. How much does each worker receive each week?

47) Arrange in order of size, starting with largest

$\frac{8}{11}$, $\frac{3}{4}$, $\frac{18}{25}$, $\frac{11}{15}$

48) Decrease 16 by 15%

49) Patrick had a collection of 300 marbles. He gave $\frac{5}{12}$ of the collection to his brother Harry and $\frac{3}{10}$ of the collection to his friend James. How many marbles did he give away altogether?

50) Write $\frac{7}{18}$ as a decimal